印度与世界：
对融入世界新模式的认识

［印］苏库马尔·莫拉里塔兰 著
(Sukumar Muralidharan)

刘小雪 译

India and the World :
Understanding New Modes of Engagement

社会科学文献出版社
SOCIAL SCIENCES ACADEMIC PRESS (CHINA)

作者：苏库马尔·莫拉里塔兰

苏库马尔·莫拉里塔兰是德里的一位新闻自由撰稿人。他有二十多年平面媒体的从业经历，包括最近一次就职于印度《前线》杂志，职位是副主编。在此之前，他还在从属于印度报业托拉斯的孟买的《印度商业》以及班加罗尔的《德干先驱报》工作过。

他曾在德里的印度国立伊斯兰大学（Jamia Millia Islamia）尼赫鲁中心做过一年的访问学者。作为一名新闻工作者，他负责报道、撰写和编辑的文章涉及科技、商业和经济及政治国际问题等众多领域。

研究受到印度乐施会的支持。

摘　要

　　由于 2000 年以来经济增长表现突出，印度若干年前就被归为新兴经济体，世人也日渐认可它是一个正在形成中的全球性大国。印度的官员们因此更加自信，商人们也有了一种"无所不能"的劲头，但实际上印度内部还没有达成政治共识，特别是那些冲突频发的地区似乎根本就没有分享到印度上升为全球大国的荣光，贫穷、营养不良仍在那里肆虐。印度的统计程序本来就一直饱受争议，而最近又有了结论性的证据，即弥漫在千年之初的乐观情绪认为印度在减贫方面取得了相当大的进展，这仅是一种错觉。近些年，政府引入了一系列进步性的立法，在诸如就业和教育领域做出的财政承诺越来越多，但是这些承诺的基础并不牢固。随着 2007～2008 年国际金融危机的爆发，人们有理由担心印度经济增长的渠道会有所缩减。通胀升高令人忧虑，而深入分析导致通胀的因素表明，如果没有大的举措，政府的一些新的财政承诺将变得不可持续。在应对一些重大的全球性问题如多边贸易谈判和气候变化谈判时，印度在相关机构中扮演着重要角色。它像坚实的堡垒，反对任何企图将不平等条约强加给发展中国家的努力，因此一直被视为"正义之声"。然而，在国际裁军委员会中，它的声望在下降，在其他重要的国际舞台上，它的潜力还有待证明。市民社会的行动需要目标集中、持之以恒，唯有如此才能推动政策机构做出削减贫困人口的实质性努力。

出品：印度乐施会

目　录

1

结束虚妄，走向实际

6 月的印度，很多报章都在自豪地谈论一件事，就是印度百万富翁的人数又增长了 50%，这一增速在全球是最快的。但是印度百万富翁的绝对人数 2009 年才刚刚超过 12 万，与印度的 12 亿人口相比，又少得可怜。① 媒体重视这件事、这个数字说明它们错置了关注的重点。开展专项研究的美林财富管理（Merrill Lynch Management）虽然也谈及这件事，但侧重点完全不同。尽管世界范围内出现金融动荡，但高端人士的财富水平进一步上升了。美林分析认为，这说明印度传奇般的增长是真实可信的，它的财富并不是虚幻的泡沫，现在亚洲的富人人数和他们的财富总量已经赶上欧洲了。

只是为避免令世人误以为印度的增长仅造就了更多的百万富翁，印度中央政府在最近几个月格外认真地开始筹划增加预算投入以满足民生。8 月初，财政部部长普拉纳布·穆克吉透露，未来三年政府将支出 2.31 万亿卢比用于教育基础设施的建设，以使每个印度人都能享受受教育的权利。在此之后，政府还有两个优先领域，就是满足人民获取充足食物和享受健康生活的权利。如此高远的目标，若在 20 世纪 80 年代简直难以想象，当时政府也曾用心良苦，但最终发现自己所有减贫努力都不了了之了。20 世纪 90 年代，印度经济翻开了新的篇章，印度增长从传奇变为现实，原本难以想象的目标也具有了

---

① 在这里，"百万富翁"被定义为个人除拥有房产之外，还有不少于 100 万美元的可处置的财富。

明确实现的可能性。① 当牛津贫困和人类发展中心宣布对贫困指标进行重大调整、使之与联合国发展项目机构年度出版物《人类发展报告》相一致之后，印度在满足人民基本需求方面存在的差距就变得更明显了。在印度百万富翁人群迅速增长这条令人愉快的消息之后，紧跟着的标题显得格外令人沮丧。OPHDI 不再使用很久以来习惯的旧标准，而是启用新的更为宽泛的贫困标准来考察印度，结果发现印度最穷的 8 个邦共有 4. 21 亿人口无法获得最基本的生活保障。实际上，仅这 8 个邦的贫困人口就已经超过了非洲 26 个最穷的国家人口的总和。与印度相比，非洲的贫困人口密度更高，但印度仅这 8 个邦的贫困人口规模就更大。②

---

① 参见财政部部长在克拉拉邦的讲话《普拉纳布说，中央政府下一个目标就是解决人民的健康与温饱问题》，《印度教徒报》2010 年 8 月 9 日，第 10 版，网址：http：//www. thehindu. com/2010/08/09/stories/ 2010080956811000. htm。
② 可参阅笔者与 OPHDI 研究报告的首席作者进行的访谈，《媒体的噱头与新印度的现实》，《印度教徒报》2010 年 7 月 20 日，第 12 版，摘自 8 月 9 日相关文章，网址：http：//www. thehindu. com/o-pinion/interview/article523817. ece。更详尽的内容可从 OPHDI 的网站上获得，网址：http：//www. ophi. org. uk/policy/multidimensional－poverty－index/。

贫困与全球呼声

这是短短 6 个月以来为印度决策者拉响的第二遍刺耳的警铃了。2009 年 11 月，一个专家组在考察了印度自走上全球化和自由化道路以来其贫困的变动趋势以后认为，印度目前使用的贫困测度法，即先将城市和农村人口每日营养摄入量换算成与那一时期物价相对应的货币价值量，以此确定贫困线，然后根据同期消费物价指数的变化再向上调整贫困线，根本无法适应 1979 年以来印度经济的变化，是对现实的严重扭曲。对于新政策的盲目拥护者而言，专家的结论除个别地方外大部分都令人不满。

这种贫困测度法显然没有考虑到生产方式和消费方式已经发生的许多实质性变化，包括自给自足、生计式农业和手工业日益让位于商品化生产，公有土地资源在消失，以及其他一些新出现的情况。例如，1979 年的贫困概念里并没有包括个人或家庭的健康开支，因为那时人人都可享受公共健康服务。而今天，在印度公共健康服务体系已是一个巨大丑闻的情况下，我们就有必要修正这个自以为是的假设了。

在教育领域，最近公共教育机构接纳穷人的政策发生了一些变化。2002 年最高法院颁布条例，要求全国所有公立学校即时起为所有在校学生提供午餐。各地落实政策的情况参差不齐，凡对这一司法条例做出了积极响应的邦，入学率确实提高了，例如拉贾斯坦邦，调查显示，该地儿童入学率有显著提高。

尽管教育并没有正式纳入贫困指数需参考的一系列变量中，但它对营养的间接影响应该计入其中。

贫困家庭顾虑的是将孩子送入学校一天，就会减少他们一天的经济收入，而现在校内免费的午餐一定程度上有助于缓解他们的这种焦虑。穷人为上学所做的挣扎，不是以年计而是以天计。按照经济理论，即使教育本身是免费的，将孩子送入学校也会有机会成本，即他们因此放弃的收入，而这顿免费的午餐至少会抵消一部分这样的机会成本。

免费午餐也减轻了家庭中直接照料儿童者的负担。通常情况下儿童的照料者是母亲或者姐姐，现在她们可以参加一些经济活动来补贴家用。通过提高营养水平、减少被迫进入劳动力市场的家庭女性成员的焦虑，免费午餐计划降低了家庭为孩子提供午餐的花费，因而是一种扶贫举措。一年中在孩子在校的 180 天里，其他家庭成员可以有机会挣得更高的收入、获得更好的营养以及其他的生活便利。要看到这一举措对贫困真正的影响，可能还需要再等一代人，也就是等到今天的这一代孩子获得完整教育、最终进入社会之时。

然而，我们现在能够获得的贫困数据都是午餐计划发生积极影响之前的。国家样本调查组织（NSS）每五年才根据消费支出对贫困人口进行一次估算。最近一次的样本采集是在 2004～2005 年进行的，因而所有的结论都是围绕着这次和前两次调查，也就是 1999～2000 年和 1993～1994 年的调查做出的。

整个讨论中争议最大的是关于 1999～2000 年的数据，在那次调查中受访者需提供在三个不同时期内他们对特定生活必需品和嗜好的消费数据，即一个星期、一个月和一年。正如此后专家发现的，这样做的结果是数据从一开始就出现混乱，使得最终结果与以前的测算完全不匹配。

正因为如此，官方宣布的印度在实行经济自由化的这些年中减贫取得重大进展才引发了广泛争议。在官方的陈述中，不论是贫困人口的相对比重还是贫困人口的绝对数量，都在 1993～1994 年、1999～2000 年和 2004～2005 年这三次消费支出的调查期间有了明显下降。但有更多不反对印度的经济自由化进程，只是讨厌政府夸大其词的严肃学者，与普林斯顿的安格斯·代顿（Angus Deaton）一样，认为印度的贫困人口比例确实有所下降，但贫困人口绝对数量的减少并不明显。另一些学者如阿皮吉特·森就认为1995年以前根本就是印度减贫 "失去的十年"，因为贫困人数实际上不降反升。①

2009年11月的专家组报告提出了一个解决方案，以弥补现有贫困测度方法的不足，使之能够更接近现实。它认为，如果引入一个更为宽泛的定义，不仅包括营养水平，还包括居民其他的基本需求，例如健康、教育和住房，那么贫困的发生率就会比原来认为的更高。尽管我们还不确知两种方法的测算结果是否真的有很大的不同，但不管怎样，认为贫困人口已下降的看法没赢得多数人的认可。实际上，贫困人口是增加而不是减少了：据调查，1993～1994年贫困人口为4.03亿，而2004～2005年贫困人口达到了4.07亿。②

这些数字还是透露出一些积极信息的，至少它们表明印度的贫困人口比重确实有所下降，但是对于正承受巨大的财政压力且一直强调社会福利必须针对穷人的印度政府而言，这仍是难以接受的。由于庞大的贫困人群的存在，政府很难缩减预算补贴，特别是针对穷人的粮食补贴，因而政府财政减支计划看来将无法落实。

---

① 这些问题都被列入了一张很实用的概括性的表中，不过该表难免偏向于安格斯·代顿自己的观点。参见安格斯·代顿和瓦莱里·柯塞尔（Valerie Kozel）的论文《数据与教条：有关印度贫困问题的大讨论》，网址：http://papers.ssrn.com/so13/papers.cfm?abstractid=593864。
② 由经济学家苏勒什·丹杜卡尔（Suresh Tendulkar）主持的专家小组发表的报告可从计划委员会的网站下载，网址：http://www.planningcommission.nic.in/eg poverty.htm。

3

财政困境与对公共福利的承诺

印度承诺要让超过总人口 1/3 的贫困人群过上更好的生活，而未来几年它能够突破财政困境是实现这个目标的关键。印度是遵从"发展才是硬道理，穷人最终都会从高增长中受益"的理念，还是回到它的老路上，认为穷人才是增长的关键，而不是任其等待"溢出效应"的实现？要保证经济发展的公平和公正，就需要承认穷人才应该是增长进程中的首要力量。

从舆论来看，政府认为增长是摆脱贫困的解药，而直接与贫困开战并不能带来必然的增长。印度政府每年在联邦预算公布之前都要发布经济调查，最新一版就表现出它在哲学上的进退维谷：它谈到人类发展指数的改善是由人均收入的增长所驱动的，接着在同一段中却又相当勉强地说，"印度改善民生的努力应该跟上人均 GDP 增长的步伐"。①

在媒体经常做的有关政府的民调中常常透露出一个观点，就是"凡是对经济有利的一定是对政党政治不利的"。而经济运行好坏也只有一个参数，就是经济增长率。在台上的政党到了大选的关键时刻，总是会被诱惑着去采取一些财政上完全不负责任的做法。但媒体的结论是，这些滥用国家资源以为

---

① 印度财政部：《2009 ~ 2010 年度经济调查》，2010，第 270 ~ 271 页。很明显，如果完全依照物理学的类比来考察，增长并未有力地推动人类的发展。所有的主动力在最终转化为可使用的能源时都要遭受效率损失，但是所有的主动力都会清楚地标记它的做功效率，如火车的柴油发动机在最好条件下的效率是 50%。如果经济增长就是人类发展的动力，我们对于它的最终动能效率还不得而知。

政党谋取私利的努力最终都得不偿失，白白流失的是自由化带给印度的增长机会。

2004 年，当各大金融报刊和新闻频道都在为"闪光的印度"欢呼时，只有为数不多的世人才会相信这个。这之后，以"闪光的印度"为竞选口号的政党在全国大选中受到重挫不得不下台。这一切说明了一个事实，就是尽管印度在某些地方确实取得了辉煌的进步，但是这个国家的大部分地区仍陷落在绝望的深渊之中。

如何做才能恢复一个民主政体赖以维系的社会和经济公正的表象呢？2004 年上台的新一届政府找到了答案。由于这届政府是由国大党领导的，而这个党被摒弃在权力通道外长达十年之久，以致最初曾怀有的独一无二执掌印度的自信荡然无存，因此它选择的答案就是重拾 20 世纪 70 年代和 80 年代初期的民粹主义政策。这意味着在财政谨慎压力不断增加的同时，政府还在通过刺激农村经济来直接应对贫困问题。2005 年通过了国家农村就业保障法案（NREGA），在全国 200 个最穷的地区向每一个愿意工作的个人提供不少于 100 天的非技术劳动机会。2006 ~ 2007 财年是充分落实国家农村就业保障法案的第一年。

信息权利法案（RTI）与新的透明体制

在国大党年轻的领袖拉胡尔·甘地的呼吁下，国家就业保障计划在2008~2009年被推广至全国。计划实施这四年被认为是政党负责、官僚机构运转透明的时期。这正是信息权利法案得以通过和实施的前提，该法案是2004年上台的这届政府通过的第一个重要的法案。

很多社会团体和左翼政党就像对待工作权利法案一样，在过去十年中一直都将信息权利法案视为他们优先考虑的内容，但所有努力最终的成果仅是一系列相关的邦级立法，根本无法成为担当公共问责的有效工具。联邦政府最终在2005年通过了信息权利法案，使之适用于全国。此法案被认为具有开拓性的意义。面对此法案，官僚机构多方努力希望能够削弱条文的约束力从而维护他们的特权，但这些努力都被市民社会的有效运作挫败了。

因为有了信息透明，国家农村就业保障法案才能够获得成功，而之前类似的政策因为没有这样一个环境，所以大都不了了之了。事实上，国家就业保障计划实施的整个过程，特别是与公共信息发布相关的部分，包括受益人名单的公布、工资支付数额，都是由社会团体设计的，它们多年来一直积极推动信息权利法案的出台，而且也掌握了这类福利项目之前实施进程中存在的不足。国家就业保障计划在设计过程中就力图避免再犯这些错误，以使目标中的受益人群实现福利最大化。

相关机构在国家就业保障计划实施的头几年就对它做了一些评估，其中经济学家让·德雷兹（Jean Dreze）和他的助手们的工作最为引人注目。[①] 这些评估工作证明了该项目对乡村生活及村民们的生计有着积极的影响，同时也指出了一些需要改进的重要领域。在这些不足之中，特别值得一提的是薪酬制定过于武断，还有腐败导致资金流失随处可见。另外，德雷兹研究了官方数据，发现妇女占国家就业保障计划受益者的40%～44%，在泰米尔纳德邦甚至高达81%，但要进一步提高妇女的参与比例就需要解决儿童看护设施短缺问题。

项目实施中存在的大多数问题都可以认为与官僚问责机制不到位有关，没有官僚问责，管理人员和基层能人得以相互勾结侵占款项，造成公共福利项目难以成功。

受国家计划委员会的指派，一家独立的研究机构对国家就业保障计划进行了一次更为正式的评估，结果发现项目实施结果喜忧参半，但还是有理由对它抱有希望。报告的观点透露出一种忧虑，就是担心计划不能为农村地区创造长久的就业机会。计划的实施的确提高了目标地区人群的营养水平，但它无助于长期解决农村的就业问题。这就带来了两个问题。一是已陷印度城市于瘫痪中的移民潮仍然无法遏制，这一失败尤其令人关注。[②] 另一个需要注意的问题就是，鉴于国家就业保障计划长期存在，它所创造的购买力与农村地区生产物资的积累不相匹配。

这些问题目前为止还没有引起政府的足够重视，但是会影响农村促进就业战略的有效性。自从很久之前自由化作为一项国策开始实施以来，印度政府就不再支持任何扩大乡村福利支出的举措，这是因为政府优先考虑的是削减预算赤字。国家负债累累，通胀肆意攀升，赤字就是造成这一双生弊端的主要因素。

---

① 参阅由让·德雷兹和他的助手完成的两篇文章，分别发表在2007年7月27日和2009年2月27日的《前线》杂志上，网址：http://www.frontlline.in/fl2414/stories/20070727001804100.htm，http://frontline.in/fl2604/stories/20090227260410100.htm。

② 人力资本应用研究所：《全印就业保障计划评估报告：来自20个区的调查》，德里，2009，可从网上获取，网址：http://www.planningcommission.nic.in/reports/genrep/repNREGA03－08－2009.pdf。

有一种观点认为，对农村地区公共工程项目的财政投入不会导致通货膨胀的压力，即使有，也不大，而且还是暂时的，它只会造成预算的压力。整个 20 世纪 90 年代，政府和它的代理机构存储的缓冲储备粮已经多到令它们头疼的地步。由于远远超过了预定的储备量，这些余粮的维护成本就成为公共支出的一大负担。因此有人就提出，在这种情况下，政府可以以发放余粮的方式向参与公共项目的农民支付薪酬，这样做既达到了提高乡村居民营养水平的目的，又得以坚持财政的现实主义目标。如此一来，随着农村公共项目的扩大，多余的粮食储备将大幅减少，国家的粮食补贴也会因此降低。换句话说，降低粮食库存可以节约资金，但是这些资金远不能弥补向农村贫困人口提供的转移支付。

与粮食一样，整个 90 年代在其他一些以满足贫困人口消费需求为目的的领域也存在着严重的产能过剩。结果人们就有了一个较为现实的期许，认为不断增加的大众消费需求，可以轻易地通过产能的提升得到满足，还不会带来任何的通胀风险。

应对通胀

　　如果说正是出于对财政赤字的顾虑，印度政府才会去抵制这个正变得日益难以抵制的需求，那么从其他方面它也得到了一些来自经济教条之外的警示——印度在整个 20 世纪 90 年代以及 21 世纪初期那几年的增长经验传递出了一个完全不同的并且与社会福利概念完全相反的理念。那些年，矛盾的是，政府的粮食储备不断增加，与此同时农业的增长率却在直线下降。换句话说，过度供给的出现有可能是通过压抑贫困人口的粮食需求实现的。从经济自由化开始直至最近这二十多年来，农业一直处在低增长的状态，但同时这也是一个低通胀时期。

　　人均粮食可获取量不断下降，大宗消费物资的库存不断上升，同时通胀率一直保持较低水平，为什么这些现象能够在印度同时并存，迄今还没有一个可靠的经济理论能够对此做出解释。不过自由化这些年的低通胀经历还可以从另一个角度来解读，即它很可能是粗暴地压制低收入人群的生活水平的结果。

　　为了确保它自身存在的合理性，农村就业计划还需要面对它对劳动力市场造成的另一个严重的伴生影响。大量剩余劳动力的存在可以保证农业资本家以较低的工资支出雇到他所需的农业工人。而就业保障计划现在为农村劳动力提供了另一个选择，这使得农业资本家为了雇到工人不得不提高工人的工资待遇。这些农业资本家转头就会要求政府提供更高的农产品支持价格，预算赤字会因此上升，通过公共分配体系卖出的粮食的价格也会上升，总之，随着相关压力的释放，通胀率将呈螺旋式上升。

这些因素在印度农村的宏观经济运行机制内都开始发生作用了吗？没人对此能够做出权威的判断。但毫无疑问的是，通胀，尤其是发生在大宗消费物资领域的通胀已经到了令人担忧的地步。《2009～2010年度经济调查》谈到这一年"通胀水平已达两位数"，"尤其是在下半年，这个问题必须引起严重关注"。报告在其他地方也指出食品价格飞涨是由季风雨量不足和粮食减产预期所致。①

在印度这样一个绝大多数作物的生长有赖降雨、绝大部分人口的生计依靠农业的国家，季风雨量不足是一个解释粮价何以高企的常用理由。在当前情况下，我们有必要看一下在雨量确实不足的过去两年里，这个理由是否真的那么令人信服。

在2009年印度气象部门记录的降雨量只有长期平均水平的77%。但要得出雨水短缺与农业产出的关联值大小实属不易，更别说与通胀联系上。但若要使论据更充分，可与2002年做一个比较，当年全国的降雨量只有长期平均水平的81%。若再往前推，1987年降雨量与此相同，大体也只有长期水平的81%。

进一步比较可知，官方公布的1987～1988年初级产品通胀率为9.7%，2002～2003年为2.6%。《2002～2003年度经济调查》在谈到"干旱与通胀"这一问题时，认为"近年来，农业经济大体从短缺向过剩转变，变得相对更加隔离于自然界的变化。因此，尽管季风雨量不足，国内的平均通胀率依然保持着较低的水平，这都要归功于过去三年出现的粮食储备剩余"。②

但是，到了2009～2010年初级产品的通胀率就已经攀升至8.8%了，远高过2002～2003年（2.6%）的水平，与1987～1988年（9.7%）的水平已非常接近，仅是略低一些而已。

对统计数据的精确性孜孜以求的人可能会要求解释，2009年（77%）与

---

① 印度财政部：《2009～2010年度经济调查》，第3页和第64页。
② 印度财政部：《2002～2003年度经济调查》，第80页。

2002 年和 1987 年（81%）的降雨量仅有 4 个百分点的不同，何以通胀率会有如此大的差距？现在问题不是关联值大小难以确定，而是在降雨量、农业产出和市场行为之间根本就没有关系——连一个近似值都找不到。

用粮食储备情况的变化也无法解释这个矛盾，因为剩余，也就是富裕之后的尴尬，是发生在 2009 年干旱之后，至少之前没有这么明显。截至 2003 年 7 月 1 日，也就是季风雨量不足的 2002 年后的一年，印度粮食集团与其他官方机构掌握的储备总量是 3520 万吨。可与之做比较的是 2010 年 7 月 1 日，当时这些机构总的粮食储备为 5780 万吨。

7 月 1 日是一个农业周期的起点，因为这一天全印的种植者们都开始为下一年的收成播种了。这一天印度粮食储备量建议保持在 2690 万吨。由于 2008 年发生的世界粮食价格危机，在此基数上，印度又额外增加了 200 万吨大米和 300 万吨小麦的战略储备额度。[①] 而到了 2009 年 7 月 1 日，在此时点上印度的粮食储备已经几乎是推荐量的两倍。此后的事情众所周知，就是印度储备粮由于缺少存储空间正在腐烂。[②]

数据，尤其是来自官方枯燥的统计手册中的数据，从来就不能对众多现实生活问题提供充分的解释，也更无法解释生产活动完全有赖于地区降雨、土壤品质、灌溉系统及其他一些要素的农民可能面对的选择。但是，仅从政府主张的事实与官方发布的年度《经济调查》所罗列的数据之间存在的出入来看，2002 ~ 2003 年政府宣称的印度经济已不再受季风雨量变化的影响，显然不是事实。

如果按照《经济调查》将 2002 年的后季风情形定义为"过剩"的话，那么这同样也适用于情形有过之而无不及的 2009 年。但是如果说 2003 年是因为有了"剩余"才足以抵御通胀，那么拥有更多剩余的 2010 年则被认为是

"余"得还不够多。如此看来，《经济调查》真是太懒了，而且在学术上也不够诚实，所以才会随意地将2010年发生的食品通胀归因于季风雨量的不足。

国家就业保障计划有助于释放农村人口压抑已久的消费需求，导致食品通胀率开始上升，这只能作为现阶段的一个假设，还需要做进一步的调查。因为对农村就业的财政投入并没有显著提高资产的生产率，结果就是农村贫困人口购买力的上升并没有辅以社会产品的增加。国家就业保障计划向农村贫困人口提供了带薪的工作机会，增加了他们的谈判实力，使他们得以抬高大农场主乐于支付的报酬水平。

图1表明了农村的发展性支出在过去这些年中的变动趋势。很明显，在2002年旱灾过后，发展性支出并没有大的提高。而那时的政府如果将保护农村贫困人口的购买力视为自己的首要任务，那么提高发展性支出就是顺理成章的事。与之相对应的是，自实施国家就业保障计划以来，中央和地方对农村地区发展的整个预算承诺提升了一个等级。由此可以直接做出一个推论，就是国家就业保障计划在提升农村地区购买力方面确实部分达到了它预期的目标。

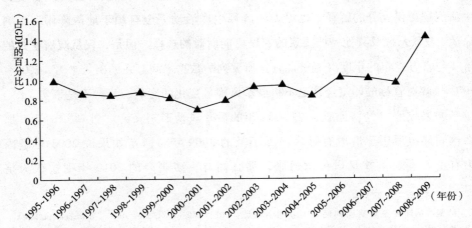

图1　中央政府与各邦政府加总的农村发展性支出（经常性与资本性支出）的变动趋势

生产能力不能与购买力保持一致，意味着在自由化初期的这些年中一直锁在瓶中的通胀魔鬼现在又被释放出来了。如果过去仅是一个序幕，那么官方对通胀威胁的最可能的反应就是首先削减用于农村公共项目的预算资金。

世界粮农组织（FAO）发现，实现农业高增长、增加人均粮食供给、提高公共医疗开支始终都是减少贫困和营养不良的成功策略。① 自从经济自由化开始以来，这些条件印度都没有满足。事实上，这期间印度做的正相反。

印度究竟从哪里获得自信，认为它在消灭贫困方面正取得实质性的进展？我们不得而知。是什么支撑着印度决策机构的乐观情绪？我们也找不到任何现成的官方解释。但是官方的发言人总是能够迅速地对相反信息提出质疑，同时回避他们认为不利的证据。尽管如此，不可否认的是，印度在经济自由化以来的这二十年中实现的增长速度是形成印度这种少见的自得情绪的一个最重要的原因。如果说前十年还看不出自由化的结果，那么到了后十年"印度大放光芒"的信念也就日益明确了。

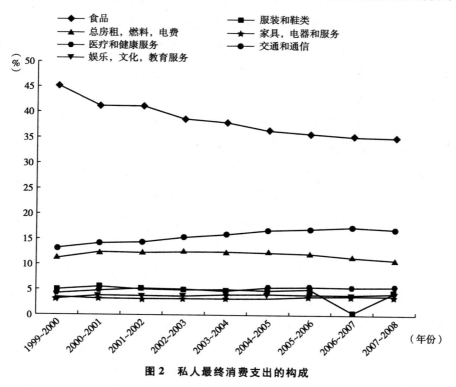

图2　私人最终消费支出的构成

---

① 可参阅 2009 年版的世界粮农组织年度报告《不安全的世界粮食现状》中的"消灭饥荒"一章。

如果细究增长的动力所在，那么很明显主要动力都来自投资率的增长。整个消费支出占 GDP 的比重有所下降。政府的消费支出占比保持在一个相对的高位上，而私人消费支出的构成出现了重大变化，属于生活资料的传统产品包括食品、衣服和居所在消费支出中总的占比大幅下降。而私人最终消费增加的部分都是些中上阶层人群感兴趣的产品和服务，例如交通设备和通信、健康医疗服务及娱乐文教服务等。

这一特殊的增长模式就是在印度收入和财富不平等越来越严重的背景下发生的。①这二者实际上是紧密联系在一起的。这是从经济增长不可避免地与一国经济结构相关联这一古老的真理中得出的推论。经济学家 Kaushik Basu 在最近发表的一篇论文中对此有所论述："GDP 高速增长的实现主要依赖比重小却产值增速奇高的富裕人口，中等收入人群虽增势不错，但与前者相比还不够迅速；而剩下的 20% 的国家底层人口简直就是在以龟速增长了。这也能说明贫困问题的走势。以低于贫困线的相对人口数量衡量，贫困正在下降，但是下降的速度之慢令人难以接受。"②

自全球化成为国策以来，印度在减贫方面的表现乏善可陈。能否认为不断扩大的不平等是造成这个问题的关键性因素呢？在这里有一个事实需要澄清：尽管印度的不平等在加剧，但就业机会不可否认的增加还是产生了收入和财富的溢出效应。后面还要对这个问题详加论述，但需要明白的是这种增长模式以及它对社会和政治稳定带来的影响，都对印度融入国际社会产生了影响。

第一个影响就是印度不愿意在国际机构中公开支持公平与公正这一普世价值，因为一旦实施这些理念，例如要求全球资本流动保持透明，短期内有可能损害到印度的增长前景。第二个影响就是用"人不为己，天诛地灭"的

---

① 目前为止，学者们在这个问题上已具有了一定的共识，可参考 Himanshu 做的实证分析《近期贫困与不平等的变动趋势：一些初步的研究结果》，《经济与政治周刊》2007 年 2 月 10 日，第 497 ~ 508 页。

② Kaushik Basu：《印度的两难困境：在全球化的世界政策制定的政治经济学》，《经济与政治周刊》2008 年 2 月 2 日，第 54 页。

理念在道义和政治上指导印度参与国际社会的活动。在大多数重要的全球性谈判中印度都扮演着发展中世界领导者的角色，现在它更渴望的是成为毋庸置疑的一个霸主，而不仅仅是同类中位居前列的那一个。

印度在它参与的大多数国际事务中已显现出这种态度的转变，但表现最明显的还是它对周边事务的处理。国内时常有一种论调，认为印度应该忘记它的全球野心，而以建设性的方式专注于周边地区，真诚地将历史强加给它的负担甩在脑后，积极推进地区合作。但是，在"印度大放光芒"的主流国策中，这一想法的影响力实在太微弱了。

6

可靠务实地参与全球事务的几个最初步骤

近一时期在一些全球压力团体，如由印度、巴西和南非组成的三方对话论坛（IBSA），为应对哥本哈根气候框架谈判而成立的巴西、南非、印度和中国四国集团（BASIC），以及由巴西、俄罗斯、印度和中国组成的金砖四国（BRIC）中，印度表现非常活跃。这些压力团体的出现有助于它的成员在一些多边场合形成共同立场，因为以往在这些场合发达国家利益总是第一位的，而发展中国家对发达国家释放出来的压力又缺乏应对手段，使得发达国家可以利用双边贸易和捐助威逼利诱发展中国家放弃不同的谈判主张。2003 年 9 月在墨西哥坎昆召开的第五次世贸组织部长会议为这些压力团体的出现奠定了基础。当时发达国家试图跟从前一样强行通过它们会前就拟定的完全体现了它们自己意志的声明和决议，印度、巴西和南非这次走到了一起，列出了它们自己的谈判清单，要求美国和欧盟必须在农业领域满足它们提出的条件，否则全球贸易谈判就不会取得任何重大的进展。①

在之后的坎昆峰会上它们依然保持着紧密联合态势，甚至吸引到了其他一些对保护弱势农民和扩大农业出口市场都感兴趣的国家。别说泰国、阿根廷和其他国家了，就是巴西、南非和印度之间，也存在着固有的巨大差异，使得它们在坎昆的共同事业以及它们的联合都很不稳定，谈判对方稍有让步

---

① 参考笔者的文章，题目是《发展中的不合作》，发表在 2003 年 9 月 12 日出版的《前线》杂志上，网址：http：//www.frontline.in/fl208/stories/2003912001804500.htm。

都有可能导致这边阵营的瓦解。美国和欧盟在农业补贴方面的顽固不化反倒成为压力团体之间的一种强黏合剂，印度、巴西和南非的联合经受住了冲击，赢得了声望和信誉。

这一团体自此继续拓展它们的合作领域、提升合作强度。IBSA 现在已成为在众多国际论坛上对发展中国家有着深远影响的团体，它也已经成为一个半正式的政治团体，定期举办峰会讨论多边事务。最近一次在巴西首都举办的峰会上，IBSA 同意一起研发一颗卫星，并密切协调它们在一些重大的国际问题如联合国改革、气候变化和世界贸易谈判上的立场。

另一成员不同、关注目标也完全不同的团体的出现则非常偶然，完全是基于高盛公司一名经济学家在 2001 年做出的一个牵强预测。他预测巴西、俄罗斯、印度和中国这四个人口加起来占世界 40%、土地面积占 1/4 的国家，将在 2050 年取代今天所有的强国，成为世界经济的主导力量。对于四国而言这一预测极具诱惑力，而且来得也适逢其时——当时目睹美国一极超霸、单边盛行并总想以虚假借口入侵他国，各国深感疑惧，却又无从诉说。

美国入侵伊拉克之后不久，上海五国组织——在 1996 年塔利班控制阿富汗全境之后由俄罗斯、中国和三个原苏联中亚共和国倡导成立的一个团体，就吸收了乌兹别克斯坦，正式更名为上海合作组织（SCO）。尽管印度最初由于上海合作组织毫不掩饰它的战略目的，即挑战美国霸权，因而对这个组织不冷不热，但最终它还是在 2005 年成为上海合作组织的观察员，目的是对它所关注的两个目标阿富汗和巴基斯坦有所牵制。

金砖四国（BRIC）在一系列共同目标下既融合了一点上海合作组织的东西，又增加了一点 IBSA 的东西，以致很难界定和描述最终出现的这个集合体。当印度与美国结成新的战略伙伴关系，而它也被日益塑造为平衡中国不断上升的地区和全球影响力的一支力量时，金砖四国定义上的含糊性也就更甚了。但是，在很大程度上由于俄罗斯的倡议，金砖四国开始在 2006 年讨论将四国集团升格为一个正式的组织，到了 2009 年四方在叶卡特琳堡召开了首次领导人峰会。

会后四方通过了一个十六点声明，提出为建立一个更稳定的国际秩序各方应首先改革现行的国际金融机构。它还提到在这些国际机构高端委员会的组成中应增加转型经济体和发展中经济体的发言权。声明还鲜明地指出美元作为事实上的国际储备货币已经难当重任了，呼吁建立一种更稳定、更加可预测、更加多样化的国际货币体系。[1]

鉴于当前的国际问题十分复杂，金砖四国中的一部分很快又与 IBSA 三国集团联系上了，也就是中国与原来的三国集团结合在一起形成了另一个地区间的集团，这个新集团又被称为 BASIC。

当 IBSA 2010 年 4 月在巴西利亚第一次审议和拟定未来发展行动纲要时，这三个集团都已开始运转了。之后很快金砖四国公开阐明了它对构建国际经济秩序的想法。接着就轮到 BASIC。这时南非已回到了会议桌前，俄罗斯却收拾行囊离开了，好为在气候变化谈判中具有举足轻重地位的中国腾出地儿。

---

① 选择俄罗斯总统的官方网页，网址：http://archive.kremlin.ru/eng/text/docs/2009/06/217963.shml，也可参见 2009 年 7 月 17 日《印度教徒报》头版的报道《金砖四国应为一个更美好的世界秩序的建立创造条件》，网址：http://www.hindu.com/2009/06/17/stories/2009061759641000.htm。

7

在不同的论坛保持原则的一致性

印度一直希望这些论坛能够独立运作、各司其职。在它的设想中，IBSA是一个民主论坛，作为一个洲际组织它能为更广大的人群代言。这里的潜台词就是，三个民主国家，每个都声称代表了它所在的大陆，那么在它们联合起来与主导着全球经济事务的西方列强打交道时，就会有更大的公信力。印度人并不确信金砖组织能够成为它实现更大的地缘政治野心的工具，这主要是因为中国也在其中。尽管第一次金砖国家首脑峰会通过的十六点声明恰如其分地谈到了联合国的改革，在礼节上也对印度在国际组织中提升位次的渴望表示了尊重，却在明确支持印度入常问题上止步不前了。中国很明显认为，只要印度和自己以及巴基斯坦还有未决的争议，那么印度就不可能被授予安理会的永久性席位。

四月峰会之后在被问到如果地区组织中一些自动停止运作、一些更清楚地界定它们的成员，那么这些重合的地区组织是否就能够提高它们的运行效率时，印度总理曼莫汉·辛格明确地表明这些组织各有存在的必要："IBSA有它自己的特点。它代表着三个大陆，三种民主。金砖集团最初仅是高盛公司制造出来的一个概念，而我们现在所做的就是赋予它生命。"[①]

但是通过这些论坛究竟要达到什么目的呢？2005 年在香港举行的部长会

---

① 《总理反对合并 IBSA 和 BRIC》，《印度时报》，德里，2010 年 4 月 17 日，引自 8 月 12 日的文章，网址：http：//timesofindia. indiatimes. com/india/PM – against – merger – of – IBSA – BRIC – blocs/arti-cleshow/5823437. cms。

议上，由于要刻意回避各成员的敏感问题，最终 WTO 通过了在它的历史上最缺少实质性内容的一份决议。自此以后 WTO 就好似淡出人们的视线了。之后 WTO 又错过了一次两年一度的部长会议，直到 2009 年 12 月才似乎醒过神来，在它的总部日内瓦召开了新一轮的部长会议，而这只是为了郑重地实践它对成员所做的一项承诺。因而，与会方都很清楚，会议不会开展新的谈判，而只会评估进展、重申承诺。

2009 年 9 月，印度举办了一场由 WTO 重量级成员参加的会议，意在彰显各方对自由贸易的共同信念，同时这也可以看做发展中国家的一种姿态，表明它们愿意成为多边谈判的利益相关方。

如同预料中的一样，世贸谈判没有取得进展，因为 2008 年 7 月草拟的谈判意向涉及三个最具争议的领域：农业，非农市场准入（NAMA，或者简单说，就是工业品关税）以及服务业，使得一年后的谈判从一开始就具爆炸性效果。除非所有的事情都达成一致，否则就不会有任何成果。要在这样的谈判过程中求得平衡，真的是非常艰难。工业化国家固执地坚持它们对农业的补贴以及其他扶持性政策，而印度和其他发展中国家则坚称，除非农业市场准入有所改善，否则它们是不会降低工业品的关税的。只要僵局还在——这种可能性很大，因为全球经济衰退使得贸易保护主义有所回潮，在这种情况下，IBSA 就还将继续发挥作用，除非它们中有任何一方选择与发达国家秘密达成交易。

印度和其他国家在坎昆会议期间提交的有关农业开放的建议，在协调出口导向的发展中经济体与大农场主经济体的不同利益方面做得非常成功，因为后者希望保护本国市场。印度认为它自己是属于后者的，而巴西则毫无疑问属于前者，将这两个国家联系在一起并将南非也拉进同一阵营的一个因素就是这些国家各自建立起了相对全面、多样化的工业体系，这使得它们有资格在非农产品的谈判中坚持自己的立场，直到满足它们在农业领域提出的条件。尽管各方之间潜在的差异不小，但是在坎昆会议上形成的这种团结态势延续到了香港会议上，而且还在继续，这说明它们决心确保乌拉圭回合犯过的错误不会重犯。

2009 年 9 月在德里召开的缩小版部长级会议同样不出意外地没取得多少进展。WTO 最近发布的简讯说，有 11 个小组已经建立起来，共有五个参与者，目的是探讨如何打破僵局，特别是有关农业、非农市场准入及服务贸易的谈判。印度就是这五个参与者之一，其他的还有美国、欧盟、巴西和中国。① 在这一轮讨价还价过程中，印度与巴西在 WTO 框架内的结盟会受到考验，而中国的存在更会增加合作的不可预测性。

印度和其他发展中国家在乌拉圭回合谈判中强行将农业塞进了多边谈判的议程中，作为交易的一部分，它们也不得不答应取消纺织品配额、实施新的知识产权保护规则。工业化国家在农业领域做出的让步非常空泛，以致发展中国家从中获得的好处实在有限，而印度获得的更是可以忽略不计。

自乌拉圭协定实施以来，印度的农业不仅没有在新的全球贸易环境下蓬勃发展，而且还落入了绝望的深渊。在农业的发展存在很大不确定性的时期，作为一个对很多不同的经济活动都具有司法管辖权的机构，WTO 成为人们不满和抱怨的对象，这是再自然不过的事了。在它存在的第一个十年中，WTO 被认为应对发生在印度农业领域的生计危机承担首要责任。

这个故事听起来已经不再那么刺耳，因为随着谈判僵局旷日持久，WTO 也在日渐淡出人们的视野。但是，即使是在 WTO 的鼎盛时期，同那些源于恶魔学说的故事一样，这个故事也过于夸张了些。WTO 当然可能啃食掉一部分印度农业的物质利益，但它的主要影响在于印度根本就没有得到发挥的机会。在 WTO 的主持下，印度与它的主要贸易伙伴都展开了漫长的、常常也是针锋相对的谈判，早在 2000 年印度就同意加快进度消除对进口的数量限制。从 2001 年 4 月 1 日起印度对外贸不再实行数量限制，仅征收保护性关税。

印度取消数量限制有一个前提，就是它要确保将来还可以通过关税来抑制农产品进口的飙升。直到目前，印度在 WTO 成员中还保持着最高的边界税率。因此，说 WTO 的规则是造成印度农业危机的罪魁祸首，这一说法实在没

---

① 《由印度和其他四个参与者组成的 11 个小组正在努力使多哈重现生机》，《经济时报》2010 年 8 月 4 日，网址：http://economictimes.indiatimes.com/india/news/economy/foreign - trade/11 - panels - from - india - 4 - other - nations - attempt - Doha - revival/articleshow/67258975. cmsyindu。

有根据。

抛开攻击 WTO 的那些激烈言辞，简单地审视一下它所施加的这些规则，我们会发现印度已经很好地履行了它的义务。在 20 世纪 90 年代中期，当 WTO 的谈判正处在决定性阶段时，曾有机构做过一个调查，发现若以国际价格为基准，那么印度的农业补贴根本就是负值，总体算来印度农业是国家的税源而非补贴对象。[①] 没有理由相信自那以后情况已发生任何重大变化。

印度农业之所以遭遇困境，简单地说，完全是由国内因素造成的，特别是多年来对农业投资不足，而且以往公共部门还能通过创造条件、提供刺激性政策引导私人部门提高劳动生产率，但是现在它已经变得完全不作为了。由于印度职业多样化的发展十分缓慢，国内仍有超过一半的人口以农业为生，而代际土地分割和转让又使单个农场的生存变得更加困难，在这种情况下，要实现劳动生产率的持久改善，公共机构积极参与社会间接资本的创造就显得格外重要。然而，印度政府在这方面一直没有尽到应尽的责任。

---

① Ashok Gulti、Anil Sharma：《印度农业的补贴综合征》，《经济与政治周刊》1995 年 9 月 30 日。

印度增长的第二次浪潮

大家普遍认为印度经济在 2003～2004 年进入了第二个增长高峰期，增长率接近两位数。[①] 还有一个共识就是，印度国内储蓄率的提升对这一轮高增长的贡献最大。多年为负的公共储蓄率终于在 2003～2004 年转为正值，而且从此以后一直保持着强劲的增长势头。在这个十年的初期，私人企业储蓄率的表现也可圈可点，从头四年保持在 3.75%～4.75% 一跃达到了 2004～2005 年的 7% 以上，并且将这个水平保持了下去，直到 2008～2009 年这两个储蓄率的增势才有所逆转，因为国际金融危机使私人企业的盈利能力大幅下滑，而政府出台的应对萧条的财政刺激措施又使公共部门新增了许多支出承诺。家庭储蓄率在 2003 年之后也开始上升，但稍稍落后于公共部门和私企部门。

自印度开始实施 2001 年财政责任和预算管理法案以后，公共部门的整体储蓄率就开始提升。从 2002～2003 财年开始，政府就一直努力抑制支出的增长，在随后的几年中政策的结果就有所显现了。为了安抚批评意见，支出调整的负担基本上落在了中央和地方政府的非发展性支出上。[②] 由于利率偏低，政府的债务清偿义务有所减轻。此外，国防支出的增长也相对减缓，这些都对政府实现抑制支出增长这一目标起了一定的作用。

---

① Kaushik Basu：《印度的两难困境：在全球化的世界政策制定的政治经济学》，《经济与政治周刊》2008 年 2 月 2 日。

② 这种分类划分法，即发展性支出与非发展性支出的分类，一直比较模糊，它只是用于报告政府支出的三种方案中的一种，另外两种分别是资本性支出与经常性支出、计划支出与非计划支出。

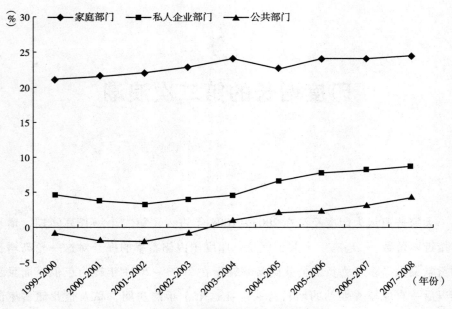

图 3　各部门储蓄率占 GDP 的比重

　　然而，中央和地方的经常性收入在这些年中都增长很快，这两级政府的税收收入占 GDP 的比重又回到了它们在 1991 年经济改革之前的水平。

　　对 21 世纪头十年里印度私人企业盈利率变化情况的综合性研究很少，但有证据表明这一时期企业的销售额增长迅速，并且在会计科目"其他收入"项下收入也非常喜人，[①] 这一切表明企业的股票投资回报率都很高，整个这一时期印度股市一直牛气冲天。

　　这一时期印度的增长轨迹还发生了另一个明显的变化，就是外国投资者对印投资兴趣上升。在十五年的时间里，印度作为直接投资和证券投资的目的地，对外国投资者的吸引力十分有限，他们对印度要么不闻不问，要么只是暂时关注一下，只是到了 2003～2004 年以后流入印度股市的外国资本才有了大幅上升。那些年直接投资增长缓慢，但 2007～2008 年和 2008～2009 年直接投资的增长特别明显。

---

① 参阅《2007～2008 年私人商业企业的表现》，《印度储备银行公报》2008 年 9 月，第 1511～1530 页。

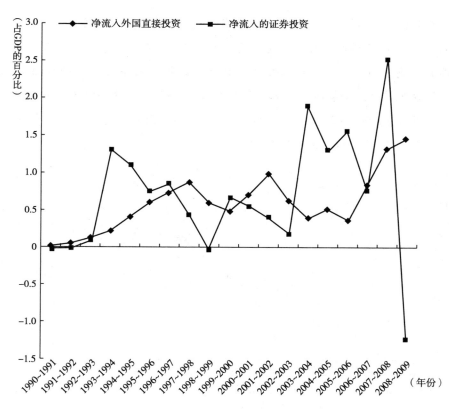

图 4　印度净流入的外资变动情况

证券投资的规模很大，流动性很强，大进大出是它的特点。所以在 2007 ～ 2008 年实现创纪录的 2. 52% 的增长之后，下一年就因为全球经济景气不再，投资者决定撤出投资，资金开始回流母国，导致当年流入印度的净证券投资为负。

而外国直接投资（FDI）的概念也非常模糊。经济学家 Chalapati Rao 做的研究发现，在他所研究的时期，有超过一半的 FDI 来自那些知名的避税港，来自毛里求斯的最多。大多数流入的 FDI 只是为了获取现有企业的股份，并不能提高企业的生产能力。印度吸收的 FDI 有超过 70% 流向服务业——特别是地产、建筑和金融服务部门，制造业吸引的 FDI 只有 20% 多一点。[①]

[①]　K. S. Chalapati Rao、Biswajit Dhar：《加快 FDI 流入印度的步伐：概念和定义》，印度工业发展研究所工作论文，2010 年 4 月。笔者非常感谢 Chalapati Rao 教授能让我有机会查阅他这篇未发表论文的初稿。

　　如果将经济增长与资产价格的变动联系在一起，我们就会发现，与 2003～
2004 年印度经济开始高增长的故事同样有趣的是，资产的价格与此同时也
始飙升。例如，股票的价格已经翻了几番。以孟买股票交易所的市值为例，
在印度这个最活跃交易所上市的企业的市值总和已从 2002～2003 年占 GDP 的
23% 上升到了 2007～2008 年的 100%。① 第二年市值就跌落下来，尽管如此，
它依然要比最初上升时要高出好几倍。

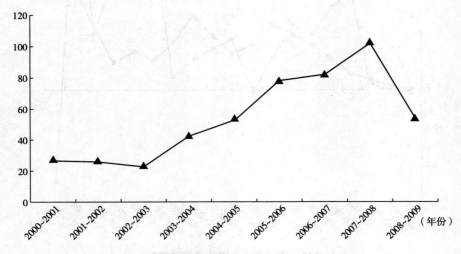

图 5　孟买交易所市值总和占 GDP 的百分比

　　我们还可以关注一下房地产市场，那里也存在着同样的趋势，但由于缺
少一个可靠的指标来衡量房产的价值，使得对市场的定性研究变得很困难。②

---

① 数据来自 RBI 的《印度经济统计手册》有关卷册。这里使用的市值数据是财年最后一天即 3 月 31
　日的数据。在某种程度上，市值都是存量的概念，而 GDP 表示的是一个流量概念，二者可能不适
　合比较，这里使用二者的比值仅仅是为了说明。
② 国家住房银行（NHB）2007 年引入了一个新的全国住房价格指标，即 NHB 房指。这个指数在
　2009 年 12 月更新过一次，显示自 2008 年下半年开始在一些主要城市住房价格有所回落，班加罗
　尔和海德拉巴尤其如此。德里和孟买的房价在 2009 年开始小幅上涨之前，整个 2008 年都没有明
　显变化。加尔各答和钦奈的房价继续上升，在二线城市如博帕尔和法力达巴德也是如此。而其他
　的二线城市如普恩、艾赫麦达巴德、斋普尔、科奇等，它们的房价在 2008 年都有明显的下降，到
　了 2009 年房地产行情也没有明显改观。（最新数据可从 http://www.nhb.org.in/residex/
　data&graphs.php 获得）不幸的是，无法获得高峰期的数据，但是根据对房地产市场从业者的调
　查，还是得出了一些估计值：德里和班加罗尔 2003～2006 年间房价涨幅大约为 26%～（转下页注）

不过，从 RBI 的数据我们可以看出，在考察期内银行对购房提供的贷款大增。从 2000～2001 年到 2006～2007 年期间"个人贷款"是整个银行信贷中增长最快的部分，其中，住房信贷又占了最大的份额。

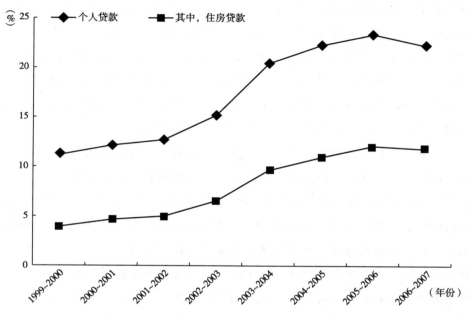

图 6　个人和住房贷款占整个银行信贷的比重（截至每个财政年度的最后一日）

如果银行自由发放信贷，很可能会在经济高增长时期引发住房价格的投机性上涨。官方的解释将住房价格飞涨归因于可处置收入的增加，而可处置收入又是伴随着大城市中专业人士收入的增加而增加的。但这样的解释并不充分，因为它无法估算出经济增长率的提升在多大程度上推高了这些专业人士的收入；它也无法说明银行部门在新的经济自由化环境下，是如何决定开展新业务、如何向收入大幅改善的专业阶层提供多种住房信贷的，以及它在其中发挥着怎样的作用。

我们还需要关注 2003～2008 年间资产价格暴涨的另一个方面。这一时期

（接上页注②）28%，而 2007 年大约为 10%～15%。（http：//www.globalpropertyguide.com/asia/india/price－history）

利率低、流动性大，信贷的取得非常容易。造成商品价格上涨的因素同样也会导致资产价格的膨胀。资产价格的上涨若超过了宏观经济基础所允许的范围，短期内可能会因刺激了资产所有者的个人消费而促进经济增长。由于流动性充足，银行和金融机构经常会为购买资产进行再融资，允许资产所有者随股东权益的增长大获其利。① 很少有研究关注所谓的"财富效应"在印度经济增长过程中的作用。但是这种贡献很可能确实存在。如果是这样的话，那么当资产价格开始回落、信贷机构为抵御资产价格的波动，开始提前为不良贷款的增加做准备时，就会发生反向的财富效应。按照相同的标准，房价如果长时间下跌，那么银行的清偿能力就会被严重削弱。

2008～2009 财年情况一直堪忧，但到了 2009～2010 年流入印度的资本又有所恢复。对于这些变化，迄今还没有一个清晰的、合乎逻辑的解释，除了这样一种解释：国际投资者在最初的慌乱期总是忙于将资本打回国内以应对险恶的经济风潮，而之后冒险精神又重回体内。印度增长的神话还在继续，鉴于它巨大的增长前景，投资者重新恢复了对印度的投资兴趣，现在印度已经成为投资者首选的海外投资地。自在 2010 年 2 月发布的《2009～2010 年度经济调查》中提出了这种解释意见，情况已经发生了很大的变化。这份经济调查做出的下述预测现在看来是如此不靠谱："随着美国、欧元区及日本已经走出了衰退、新兴经济体再现增长势头，全球经济已有回暖迹象。"② 自这份调查报告出台以来，欧元区、美国和日本的经济走势与其预测正相反。

债务负担沉重的希腊引发了这场危机，威胁到了整个欧元区的统一性和货币政策一致性，促使欧盟向其提供紧急救助，救助规模之大创历史纪录。而希腊政府迫于欧盟压力，不顾国内中低收入人群的强烈反对，开始实施紧缩的财政货币政策。美国的就业岗位也已连续几个月在减少，③ 为了将经济从

---

① 关于财富效应对消费水平的影响，可参阅旧金山联邦储备银行出版的 2007 年第二期的《时事通讯》的文章，网址：http://www.frbsf.org/publications/economics/letter/2007/el2007 - 02.pdf。

② 印度财政部：《2009～2010 年度经济调查》，2010 年 2 月在德里发布，第 124 页。

③ 参见保罗·克鲁格曼在《纽约时报》2010 年 8 月 26 日的专栏文章，题目是《这不是复苏》，网址：http://www.nytimes.com/2010/08/27/opinion/27krugman.html? hp，这篇文章总结了现实情况，反驳了美国经济正在走向复苏的观点。

衰退的旋涡中拯救出来，奥马巴政府做出了许多财政承诺，但国内就这些承诺存在很大的政治分歧，国家正因此走向政策僵局，而这很可能是危机情况下最无效的反应。日本经历了痛苦的政治变局，一位首相被迫下台，而当初他的上台曾被寄予厚望——望其将日本从长达二十年的衰退中解救出来。但是新任首相面对的挑战更多，其中既有来自党内的，也有来自日元不断升值的。日元升值被认为对美国和欧元区经济复苏非常必要，但对日本自身而言是一切不幸的根源。

将全球经济拖出衰退的旋涡，如何做才是最佳？难也好易也罢，现实是根本就没有一个统一的答案。对美国而言也许是最合理的行动，但到了欧元区和日本，可能就成了政策毒药。一方面美国和欧元区坚持认为日本应承担首要责任来振兴它的经济、为全球经济注入活力，另一方面日本自己的看法是挽救经济颓势不是它的责任，因为现在的情形完全是由美国人的大手大脚、欧盟的敏感的保护主义机制造成的。

重要国家之间的争吵声越来越高，而小国对世界经济走势的看法又少有人听，多年来讨论仅限于富国俱乐部内部，先是 G7，后来俄罗斯因为其战略力量也被接纳进来，G7 变成了 G8。现在全球政治掮客们又认为，这个特权会议大厅还应该向其他重要的利益相关方开放，否则消除世界经济不平衡就不会取得重要进展。G8 现在仍保留它的独立存在，但是每次峰会都要与包括印度、巴西、南非及其他一些国家在内的 G20 一起举办。

9

G20 和它的潜能

　　根据记录，在最近一次于 2010 年 6 月加拿大多伦多召开的 G20 峰会上，印度反对向引起发展中国家金融动荡的投机性资本征税。

　　这与印度国内的税收政策是一致的，在印度股市上获得的资本收益是免税的，股权红利也是免税的。在这个资本动荡的时代印度对这个引起全球关注的问题的态度说明它只在意保护它的短期利益，也说明这几年的增长记录遮蔽了它的政策视野，因为这些年的发展就是高度依赖短期资本的大规模流入和资产价值的飙升，特别是后者又造成了拥有持久财富的幻觉。印度政策机构不仅不敢冒险向流入的投机性资本征收实质性的税收，而且它也深知即使言辞上提及这种税收的必要性也会引起国际投资者的报复。① 随着印度的增长前景变得黯淡，官方发言人可能在谈到他们正在考虑的政策选择时会变得格外谨慎。

　　印度对 G20 的官方态度从最新一期年度《经济调查》对此的评论来看还是非常积极的。这个论坛正变得比以前更积极，2009 年将峰会从一年一度改为一年两度，2010 年也将如此。6 月的多伦多峰会之后还要在首尔举行一次峰会。

　　按照《2009～2010 年度经济调查》的说法，G20 的成员国都认为 G20 将

---

① 这里马上想到的一个案例就是 2004 年议会大选之后，大家都看出即将成立的新政府为了获得议会多数必须依赖左派政党，这时一位左派党魁发表言论，谈及他的政党反对公共部门企业私有化，立刻引起股价暴跌，以致产业巨头们要求联合政府中的其他党派一起站出来反对这种观点。

成为国际经济合作的一个最重要的论坛。

不考虑它的意图，我们关心的是 G20 在引领世界的过程中能否保持内部一致，因为这是当今世界最需要的。美国仍是全球经济唯一的支点，但现时其国内政治纷争振聋发聩，没有丝毫迹象显示它有足够胸襟带领世界采取集体行动克服当前出现的共同的经济病征。

2001 年乔治·布什政府引入了大规模减税措施，这些措施即将于 2010 年12 月 31 日到期。减税引入的时间点并不合适，当时美国刚开始实行全球军事介入，要求拥有更大的资源动员能力。所谓减税的"夕阳条款"是作为反对党的民主党和布什的共和党相互妥协的结果，双方的投机性都很强，因为双方都不确知这种属于典型的意识形态压倒常识的做法会将国家带向何方。

就在奥巴马总统正要决定是保留还是撤销布什的减税措施时，茶党运动困住了他，在该运动看来，哪怕是最轻微的后退都算是某种形式的背叛。奥巴马最初的打算，与他获得的建议大体一致，就是必须撤销对年收入超过 25万美元以上的富人的减税，同时通过降低中低收入人群的税收来刺激经济。

由备受尊重的、极富社会责任感的经济学家们为现今一蹶不振的世界经济开出的不同的药方，恰向世人展现了各国政府面对的政策选择困境是如何难解。IMF 前首席经济学家、芝加哥大学的 Raghuraman G. Rajan 就认为应该通过减少开支来削减赤字，如果必要的话，还可以有选择地增税。他还主张拥有巨额外汇储备的中国和日本政府应该重定币值。

这些建议已经被人们重复了很多年，但始终没有唤起行动。原因非常简单。在 20 世纪 80 年代中期，尽管美国贸易赤字不断扩大，但美元汇率处在前所未有的高位，美国经济几乎因此陷入危局。里根时期政府减税，增加国防开支，但他还想实现预算平衡，这根本就是南辕北辙的事，因而被称为"魔幻经济学"，当然直接后果就是高额赤字了。但是事实证明，美国经济出现的外部账户赤字是可以无限扩大的，原因就是美元是国际储备货币。

作为 IMF 首席经济学家，Rajan 作为核心人物之一，在 2006 年试图让五个最有能力扭转全球经济不平衡大局的国家一致采取最佳战略。美国、欧盟、中国、日本和沙特阿拉伯在 IMF 的协调下坐在一起进行了广泛的磋商。这里有必要用 Rajan 自己的话介绍一下会议的经过："各位对话者的反响都非常一致。这些国家都认为，贸易不平衡是不稳定的一个潜在因素，在市场发生动荡或者政客们决定采取保护主义措施积极介入之前，各国可以通过经济改革来减少贸易的不平衡。但每个国家又很快地指出为什么它自己不应该对不平衡负责，为什么由别的国家去'按下神奇的按钮'（即采取行动——译者注）让这些不平衡现象消失要比它自己做起来更容易。"①

Rajan 最后放弃了努力，灰心地回到了他的大学继续他的教职。待磋商结束时，IMF 发表了一个平淡无奇的声明，声称努力很成功：会谈为各方在一起自由坦率地交换意见创造了机会。Rajan 的评价很刻薄："这不过是一句外交辞令，意思是各方完全没有共识。"

美国认为它的外债是中国和日本以及其他一些国家储蓄过多并且愿意无限持有美国国债的结果。按照这种解释，中国才应该承担首要责任修正全球经济的不平衡，因为它长期将汇率固定在远低于它实际应该在的水平上。

而来自中国一方的反击是，美国在过去二十年里的过度消费才是引起全球不平衡的首要原因。它否认它的汇率政策与当前的问题有任何关联，坚持它还要继续以渐进的方式重新调整人民币与世界其他主要货币的汇率。中国还指出，如果它为了安抚美国重定了自己的汇率，那么很有可能它会像自 1986 年以后的日本一样陷入长期衰退。日本就是在这一年因为顶不住美国的压力使日元对美元的汇率大幅上升。

人口的变化在未来几年也会发生作用。中国人口的抚养系数，即 14 岁以下以及 65 岁以上的人口与在这年龄段之间人口的比值一直在快速下降，但到 2010 年就已经见底了，未来将会转而上升。这对它的储蓄率会有明显的影响，可能会诱使它更优先储蓄，而不是消费，因为 2020 年以后中国需要被照顾的人口会非常庞大，它必须为此做好准备。

货币升值应该被视为顺差国保持它们手中美国国债价值量不变的一项政策选择而非强制性的义务。如果债券贬值，美国将不得不提高利率以保证世

---

① Raghuraman G. Rajan：《断层：隐藏的分歧如何威胁世界经济》，《科林斯商业》，2010，第 209 页。

界仍有兴趣为它的赤字融资。这对本已深陷债务的经济是雪上加霜。

诺贝尔经济学奖获得者保罗·克鲁格曼就是最强烈地主张中国进行实质性货币改革的国际人士之一。但作为美国经济症候的解毒剂,他开出的处方还是出自传统的凯恩斯学派:通过增税实现增支,同时还有乐于买入各种债务工具为经济注入所需购买力的干预型联邦储备银行。[①] 这样一个政策如何能够与美元相对世界其他主要货币的贬值相协调,克鲁格曼并没有进行深入分析。但是如果凯恩斯的政策理念有一星半点胜出的机会,那么美元的信誉和币值的稳定显而易见是非常重要的。

按照 Rajan 所说的,中国制定政策的人从不承认对他们的指责,即他们操纵了汇率,认为他们不过是美国竞争力下降的替罪羊。在他们看来,事实其实很简单,就是如果人民币升值导致中国无法出口了,那么还会有柬埔寨、越南取代中国向美国出口,美国赤字贸易的格局依然不变,只是顺差国从中国换成了别的国家。

这样说很有道理,因为美国开始出现赤字是在 20 世纪 80 年代,当时作为另一方的顺差国是日本、石油输出国及德国(那时还被称为西德)。德国统一后就不再属于这个行列了。1986 年日元升值以及大批日本制造型企业移师美国,减少了一部分日美贸易的不平衡,但是美国的赤字继续飞涨,因为中国、一些拉美国家和一些东南亚国家成为对美贸易的顺差方。

美国的困境是结构性的,根深蒂固。就像许多类似的病症,需要整体疗法,仅仅对汇率做一个整容似的改变根本无助于解决美国制造业竞争力下降的问题,这早在 20 世纪 60 年代就已变得非常明显了,在里根时期随着金融服务业成为主导产业,(这种情况)已变得不可逆转了。

---

① 参见他的专栏文章《陷入瘫痪的联邦储备银行》,《纽约时报》2010 年 8 月 12 日,网址:http: // www. nytimes. com/2010/08/13/opion/13krugman. html? ref = paulkrugman。

10
来自气候变化的挑战和印度的反应

要驱动经济增长就离不开无生命的能源。当发展中国家开始追求发达国家的生活水平时，它们不得不面对全球共同的环境资源枯竭带来的令人沮丧的限制。如果所有国家的经济发展战略都遵循旧有模式的话，气候将会发生不可逆的变化，地球就会因此遭受巨大灾难。

气候变化是一个全球性的挑战，所有国家都应该有一个对目标的共同认识，不要被国家主义的意识形态和地缘政治暂时的优势所迷惑以致偏离长期目标。但是这也确实是刻板的国家利益最容易涉入并干扰的领域，使各方在所有相关的国际谈判中争执不下。

出于公平的理念，工业化国家由于排放了近80%的温室气体，为避免日益临近的环境灾难，它们应该承担起主要的责任。与此同时，工业化国家有责任开发新的发展范式，以替代它们原先采用的高碳密集的范式，也有义务为发展中国家提供它们用得起的基本技术和加工流程。

除了德国和英国，工业化国家少有例外地固执地拒绝这种主张，致使全球气候变化谈判陷入了实质性僵局。工业化国家继续违约，不去履行它们在1992年《京都议定书》中做出的减排承诺，甚至它所承诺的帮助筹划和资助发展中国家的减排战略，也大部分都没做到。

大致说来《京都议定书》还算是一个成功的协定，所有对日渐逼近的环境灾难起到推波助澜作用的国家，它都要求它们承担一定的具有约束力的义务。它也将"共同但有区别的责任"奉为神圣准则，同时考虑了特定国家未完成的发展的渴望以及工业化国家在全球温室气体累积过程中的历史"贡献"。但是在使日渐缩小的全球共同环境资源成为可买卖的商品的问题上，《京都议定书》完全迎合工业化国家的要求，这就为未来的谈判开了一个很不好的头。

在 2009 年 12 月哥本哈根气候峰会召开之前进行了一项针对工业化国家究竟在何种程度上实现了减排目标的调查，结果显示，几乎所有这些国家都存在严重违约。但是在哥本哈根进行的谈判没有显示出任何解决问题的诚意，会谈进程除了加深工业化国家与发展中世界的信任赤字外，再无其他收获。最终通过的声明唯一的实质性成果就是承认应该给予世界上的穷国资助，以帮助它们应对气候变化带来的挑战。这个声明被认为违背了会议的宗旨，因为工业化国家在历史上排放了太多的温室气体，与之相应的当然是承担更多的减排责任。人们原本希望工业化国家在会议上能够承认这一点。

印度是最后一刻才在这份充满了妥协的声明上签字的，声明就像一块小得可怜的遮羞布，根本无法掩饰巨大的失败。自哥本哈根会议之后，有迹象表明印度的立场已经有所改变，它不再坚持工业化国家必须首先履行它们的承诺否则发展中国家是不会履行它们的义务的。

政策界人士现在也越来越认识到一个事实，就是印度碳排放的绝对数量大得惊人。科学研究已经发现，就连早期制定的碳排放目标都太宽松，即到 2020 年将碳浓度降至百万分之 450（ppmv），在这种情况下，尽管印度的人均排放量不大，但足以成为压在骆驼身上的最后一根稻草。世界上最受尊敬的气候学家詹姆士·汉森（James Hansen）呼吁到 2020 年碳浓度需降至百万分之 350（ppmv）的水平，尽管尚未被官方的多边论坛所接受，但其影响不容忽视。

印度只是就人均排放量有唯一肯定的数量承诺。曼莫汉·辛格总理曾向德国总理默克尔保证，印度的人均碳排放量不会超过工业化国家的水平。这只不过是一个有效性和可执行性都不确定的口头承诺，但根据印度一家独立的政策研究机构"德里科学论坛"的计算，如果印度一如既往、不做改变地发展，而西方国家在减排问题上恪守承诺，那么印度的人均碳排放量在不久的将来就会超过西方的水平。①

印度需要新的战略选择。如果以公平和"共同但有区别的责任"名义继续抵制气候谈判，那么工业化国家也会继续利用印度的"不作为"来当它们"不作为"的借口，因此印度的策略被视为"躲在西方'不作为'裙下的另一个'不作为'"。② 二者结合在一起使全球谈判彻底陷入僵局。

正当其他一些发展中国家和小岛国对目前的僵局越来越感到不安时，印度最近终于意识到它应该主动采取可靠的行动。气候变化问题对于南亚国家而言尤其重要，因为它们背靠喜马拉雅山，有两个国家——孟加拉和马尔代夫——正切身感受到全球变暖的威胁。

印度在 2008 年 6 月通过了国家气候变化行动纲要。此时正是 G8 京都峰会前一周，而这次峰会的一个内容就是盘点各国在应对气候变化方面所取得的进展。因为挑选的这个时机，印度的计划引来了一些批评的声音。其中一项批评认为，印度的计划纲要缺少基线数据，最近的数据完整的一年是 1994 年。③

印度环境和森林资源部在 2010 年 5 月发布了一部更新版的印度温室气体排放详细目录，最终填补了这一数据空白。④ 研究显示，印度在全球温室气体排放者中排名居第五位，仅落在美国、中国、欧盟和俄罗斯之后。美国和中国的排放总量都四倍于印度。研究还指出，在 1994 年和 2007 年这两个被考察的年份里，印度 GDP 增长的排放强度下降的幅度超过 30%。官方的目标是到 2020 年将碳强度进一步降至 20% ~25%。

印度声称碳强度下降，这还需要更进一步的证实。难道印度采用的技术和生产流程真的就是碳排放节约型的吗？抑或这种认定的下降来源于印度自

---

① 该项研究以及其他与气候变化相关的材料都可在德里科学论坛的网页上找到，网址：http：// www. delhiscienceforum. net。

② 这段话引自美国参议员约翰·华纳，出自埃里克·普利的《气候战争》一书第一章，哈泼利昂出版社，2010。

③ Praful Bidwai：《一个可以说 Yes 的印度：一份哥本哈根及未来的气候责任的发展计划》，Henrich Boell 基金会，新德里，2009。

④ 该报告可在印度环境和森林资源部网页上找到，网址：http：// moef. nic. in/downloads/public － information/reportincca. pdf。

经济自由化以来实行了二十年的不均衡增长模式？如果所有的经济层级和社会阶级都参与到这一时期的经济增长进程中来，那么碳排放强度的下降还会发生吗？换句话说，是不是印度就要找到一种新的发展范式了，在其中所有的部门都能从增长中获益，而且还不会造成令人无法接受的、潜在的灾难性的环境后果？

印度积极支持根据《京都议定书》建立的清洁发展机制（CDM），但这并不能证明它对低碳增长道路的可行性就有很深的信念，尽管它被公认为早已经开始了这样的发展。最近一版环境和森林资源部发布的报告记录了国家行政当局已经被授权为 CDM 项目颁发证书。① 不是所有的项目都在 CDM 执行委员会登记过，但初步估计所有项目的潜力将达到 6.27 亿全球碳交易货币单位，即等量的"减排认证"。人们既看不到也摸不着这种货币，因此除了生态学界的会计师外，世人都不知道它的存在。为此，印度环境和森林资源部为这种货币标出了价格，定价相对保守，每单位只有 10 美元。

印度在全球 CDM 市场上表现突出，环境和森林资源部对此相当满意。就此事它曾指出："截至 2010 年 1 月，印度在 CDM 执行委员会登记的项目居世界第二，总共 2011 个项目中就有 478 个来自印度。"②

《京都议定书》引入的碳交易是一个非常深奥的过程，一般智商的人要理解它比理解全球金融市场还要难。它最关键的特点是反事实性。计算项目对减排的贡献根据的是如果没有这个项目，会有什么样的情况发生：如果退化的林地没有得到改善，那么会增加多少碳排放？如果土地被重新绿化，排放负担又会有怎样的变化？引入一套生产能源和混合肥料的城市固体废料处理系统，而不是任其腐烂和分解，对减少碳污染有多大贡献？

要获得 CDM 执行委员会的认证，项目必须展示对碳减排的额外贡献，而且还需证明如果没有 CDM 的资金，该项目就不具有经济意义。项目必须是自愿实施的，而不是法律强迫实施的结果。

---

① 印度环境和森林资源部：《2009~2010 年度报告》，第 269 页。
② 印度环境和森林资源部：《2009~2010 年度报告》，第 270 页。

因此，在所有的城市中心都需要建立一个市政废物处理工厂，按照 CDM 的理念，它可以成为碳信用的来源，可以在全球期货市场上卖出，而美国或者中国的污染产业可以买来充做自己的减排额度。① 美国堪萨斯城里的一个电厂的管理层一般对减排没有多少兴趣，它很可能会主动去购买印度科哈普尔的一个城市废物处理厂产生的碳信用。如此堪萨斯城的电厂运营商就可以通过补贴科哈普尔的环保产业来回避它自己的责任。

要认真对待气候变化问题，最可靠的做法就是集中精力发展新技术和新加工流程，它们环境友好，利于大众生计，且非资源密集。一个国家一旦意识到它的长期利益所在，就会认真考虑这些政策选择，而不会沉浸在这样一个由国际最大的污染者们提倡的腐败的国际碳交易网络中，不会满足于与金融机构合作去创造这个卑鄙交易的记录。重新定位印度国家的科学和技术体系使之适应新的发展范式，这在印度已经是老生常谈了，但历届政府很少拿出具体行动来实践它。

---

① 可参阅 Mark Schapiro 的重要文章《了解气候》，《哈泼斯》2010 年 2 月刊，第 31~39 页。

11

核协议之后：印度信誉下降

对核能的重视程度一直是衡量印度政策优先次序的一个指标，它一直认为发展核能是应对全球气候变化的一个不错的政策选择。受这种观点左右，印方还采取了一些战略选择，结果严重削弱了印度在发展中世界曾一度享有的合法的领导地位。

2006 年，计划委员会在十五计划中期审议报告中认为，核能部门的表现黯然无光，将它的发展不力完全归结为没能发现新的铀矿以满足核燃料的生产。这还是公众第一次听说印度缺少原子能矿物，因为自 1950 年以来印度原子能部就一直在宣传，印度有充足的资源来满足它的三阶段的核能计划，即用十年的时间要从第一阶段生产重水反应堆，过渡到第二阶段以铀为基础的快中子增殖反应堆，再到钍燃料反应堆（第三阶段）。

计划委员会总结了它对核能前景的看法，结论深具启发性："核能依旧是印度能源行业减排的重要工具。"①

核燃料循环取代碳燃料循环后，不会再有后者的各种弊端，人们对这一看法还存在争论。但这种观点，加上印度在 1998 年引爆核装置后造成的各种安全焦虑，使印度随后几个月的外交努力都围绕着如何在发展核能的同时，又能够在国际条约约束下不失灵活地建立起毁灭性核弹药库进行。

---

① 计划委员会：《十五计划中期评审报告》，德里，2006，第 339 页，网址：http：//www. planning-commission. nic. in/plans/mta/midterm/english – pdf/chapter – 10. pdf。

2005 年 7 月，曼莫汉·辛格总理访问美国，同意与美国总统签署一项联合声明，这意味着印度有核国家的地位被承认。曼莫汉·辛格和乔治·布什签署的联合声明称印度"是一个拥有先进核技术的负责任的国家，它应该获得与其他国家一样的好处和收益"。事实上，这为印度制造了一个处在"有核"与"无核"国家之间的特殊地带。就这样，印度和美国在国际地缘战略的版图上制造了一个原本不存在的点，而印度因为这个外交创新达到了它的目的。

2006 年 3 月，布什访问印度，借着这个机会双方打算完成协议的最后谈判工作。如果说已签署的协议能够平息由原子能部内部主张片面限武论者所引起的焦虑，那么它所引起的国际反响就是另一回事了。巴基斯坦的外交部部长阴沉沉地警告说，整个核不扩散条约（NPT）将会就此解体，因为其他国家迟早也会效仿印度。

印度与美国的关系也引起了各界的怀疑，包括那些从不属于敌对方的国家。例如，伦敦《卫报》的社论评论说，印度和美国的核协议"破坏了规则，会招致其他国家的效仿"。它又更形象地指出，该协议就像"某人坐在酒吧高脚凳上宣传戒酒"一样。社论接着说，印度人对这项由自己推动的交易可能会感到很欣慰，但是也很有可能朝鲜和伊朗看到了会流露出"会心的微笑"，因为协议也给它们带来了希望。①

在布什访印之前，《纽约时报》就曾观察到，排除虚幻的泡沫，总统这趟印度之行的成果就是签署了这个影响极坏的核协议。随着协议的最终签署，《纽约时报》的评论变得更辛辣了，"布什现在成了伊朗最好的朋友"。他对伊拉克的军事打击，理由牵强、证据脆弱，最终结果不过是将这个国家变成了它的伊斯兰卫星国。正当美国计划将伊朗的案子提交给联合国安全理事会以便采取进一步行动之时，布什与印度新近达成的交易却传递出一个完全相左的信息。全球一致反对伊朗的核项目，伊朗便把瓦解这个共识的希望寄托在令全世界都相信，西方的错误在于它在核问题上持有双重标准。有鉴于此，

① 《布什和炸弹》，《卫报》2006 年 3 月 4 日。

美国与印度的这份协议就相当于布什送给德黑兰的一份厚礼了。①

自那以后，印度经历了曲折的道路才最终收获了一份核协议，既满足了它的核野心，又安抚了它的核焦虑。布什政府为了让协议获得国会批准也付出了巨大的努力，包括在国际原子能机构重复投票反对伊朗，以及反对不结盟运动形成的集体共识，而印度曾是不结盟运动的发起者，并且还一度是领导者。在全球裁军谈判中，印度现在被认为是一个闯入者，一个为了追求国家安全而不惜牺牲长期原则的国家。

---

① 《伊朗最好的朋友》，《纽约时报》2006 年 3 月 5 日，社论版，网址：http://www.nytimes.com/2006/03/05/opinion/05sun1.html？r=1。

12
形象问题

现在到访印度的人都可以感受到在印度人身上有一种新的咄咄逼人的自我肯定的情绪，他们表现得非常自满，认为"我们印度已经站到了世界舞台上，在任何一个全球性的委员会的主桌边都应该有我们的位置"。但也有人认为现在欢呼还为时太早，不过他们的声音没人听到。还有看法认为，在印度这样一个国家，贫穷随处可见，社会又四分五裂，真不该这样自满。但这样的看法也没有人去留意。与此同时，来自过去、源自心底的声音仍然被过时的思维定势锁住了。

总的来说，公民社会团体对这种新的自满情绪持批评态度，但是它们对内部的这些不同意见也没有给予一定的关注。由印度主办的、可以称为一场盛大的"社交晚会"的英联邦运动会已接近尾声。在整个举办的过程中发生了太多令人着急上火的事，但这场盛会看来还是为印度的国家名誉带来了一点积极的影响。不过经济上的影响就是另一回事了，因为没有证据表明，为举办这次运动会而进行的如此大规模的公共投资能对私人部门产生任何积极的附带效益。印度为举办英联邦运动会而投入的人力成本和社会成本尚不得而知。按照信息权利法案的要求披露出来的一些信息显示，德里和更高一级的联邦政府挪用了本应用于残障人士的社会福利资金用于建设运动会场馆。①

---

① 参阅《运动会挪用 74.4 亿卢比本应用于贱民的资金》，《印度时报》2010 年 7 月 16 日，第 1 版，网址：http://timesofyindia.indiatimes.com/city/delhi/Rs - 744cr - dalit - fund - diverted - for - games/articleshow/6173912.cms。

同期国际媒体的报道都认为印度只顾向世界强国目标高歌猛进，却忘记了自己身边的穷人和弱势人群。[①]

在离英联邦运动会开幕还有不到一个月时，运动会的准备工作仍一团乱麻，印度行政当局因此备受指责。官员腐败渎职的传闻满天飞。人们担心这场印度在国际舞台上的处女秀会最终演变为一出悲剧——过度膨胀的野心在坚硬的现实面前被撞得粉碎。最后虽然印度总算避免了这样的尴尬，但是还有许多难题在前方等着它。

---

① 《"大放光芒"的印度让它的穷人为英联邦运动会买单》，《卫报》2010 年 7 月 11 日，网址：ht-tp：//www. guardian. co. uk/world/2010/jul/11/slum – school – india – commonwealth – games。

India and the World:
Understanding New Modes of Engagement

Sukumar Muralidharan

Disclaimer

Author: **Sukumar Muralidharan**

Sukumar Muralidharan is a freelance journalist based in Delhi. He has had twenty years of experience in the print media, including most recently, as Deputy Editor in Delhi of India's *Frontline* magazine. Prior to this, he has worked with the Press Trust of India, *Business India* in Mumbai, and *Deccan Herald* in Bangalore.

He was for one year, a visiting professor at the Nehru Centre, Jamia Millia Islamia, Delhi. As a journalist, he has had reporting, writing and editorial responsibilities in areas like science and technology, business and economics, politics, and international affairs.

Abstract

From being classed as an "emerging" economy for many years, India has, partly on the back of its robust growth performance since the early-2000s, earned recognition as an global power in the making. This is reflected in a new spirit of assertive self-confidence within offiial circles and a vigorous "can-do" attitude within India's business community. Internal political consensus though, seems elusive and India's many regions of endemic conflict show little sign of sharing in the drive towards global power status. Poverty and under-nutrition remain areas of serious concern. Though procedures of statistical estimation have been contentious in recent times, there is now conclusive evidence that the optimism of the early years of the millennium, that a dent had been made in poverty, was misplaced. A host of progressive legislation has been introduced in recent years, backed up with seemingly solid fical commitments in areas such as employment and education. But the foundations remain infirm and since the global financial meltdown of 2007 – 08, there have been grounds for worry that the sources of India's economic growth have themselves become rather narrow. Inflation remains a worry and a deeper analysis of its causes might indicate that some of the new fiscal commitments may be unsustainable without other tough decisions being made. India remains a major presence in global councils dealing with issues of consequence, such as multilateral trade and climate change. From being a bulwark against efforts to impose inequitable agreements on the developing countries, India has of late been seen as a voice for positive change. The country's stature in global disarmament councils though, stands diminished and its potential to contribute positively in most other forums still remains to be proved. Focused and sustained civil society action could nudge the policy establishment towards options that mean a positive difference for the world's poor.

Produced by: Oxfam India

Contents

1

Where pretence ends and reality begins

Headline news in much of the country's media in the month of June, blazoned a 50% increase in the number of millionaires in India. This was among the sharpest rates of increase that any country had witnessed. And yet with all this, the total number of millionaires in India in 2009 stood at just over 120, 000, a paltry number for a country of 1. 2 billion people. [1] If the importance given to a matter involving this number should seem an index of skewed priorities, the point as emphasised by Merrill Lynch Wealth Management, which carried out the study, was different. Despite the financial turbulence in the world economy, levels of wealth among high-net worth individuals had increased. This pointed to the sound underpinnings of the growth story, said Merrill Lynch, adding for reassurance that India's wealth is not a bubble, since "Asia has caught up with Europe in terms of its high-net worth population and their wealth".

Just in case it were to be thought that India's growth story is just about the creation of millionaires, the Union Government has over recent months been showing great seriousness of intent in increasing budgetary commitments towards basic human needs. Early in August, Finance Minister Pranab Mukherjee spoke of a possible outlay of Rs 2. 31 billion (Rs 2, 31, 000 crore) over three years to create the infrastructure that would make the right to education a reality for all Indians. Following this, the next two priorities of the Government he said, would be to make the rights to food and health operative. This level of ambition he said, would have been beyond imagination in the 1980s when the Government, despite best intentions, found itself stymied in all efforts to directly address poverty. What had made the unthinkable a distinct possibility was the turning of a page in the 1990s, which made India's contemporary and ongoing growth story a reality. [2]

Just how farIndia needs to go in terms of basic needs fulfilment became starkly clear when the Oxford Poverty and Human Development Initiative (OPHDI), announced a significant reformulation of the measure of poverty, which will be integrated into the twentieth edition of the U. N. Development Programme's authoritative annual publication: the Human Development Report. The headlines here, coming soon after the cheerful news on India's millionaires being a fast-growing tribe, were distinctly unflattering. Working with a wider definition of poverty than has so far been customary, the OPHDI found that the eight poorest states of India have no fewer than 421 million people deprived of the basic requirements of a decent life. Indeed, the number of the poor in just these eight Indian states is higher than in the 26 poorest countries of Africa. The intensity of poverty in Africa is greater; but its magnitude in just eight states of India is wider. [3]

Poverty and global voice

This was the second rude wake-up call for the Indian policy establishment in just over six months. In November 2009, an expert group tasked with ending the long-running argument over poverty trends since India stepped on to the pathway ofliberalisation and globalisation, came up with an answer that was, from the perspective of the new policy orientation and its partisans, good in some respects, but bad in most. Poverty measures, the Expert Group admitted, had been badly askew in failing to address the vast changes in economic realities since 1979, when a "poverty line" was fixed in terms of a daily nutritional intake for both the rural and urban population. This was then converted into a monetary equivalent using prices applicable at the time. Ever since, the poverty line in its monetary value, has been updated annually using the relevant consumer price index.

This method obviously fails to capture the many material changes that have taken place in production and consumption patterns, including the increasing dependence upon commodity exchange rather than subsistence farming or payments in kind, the erosion of common property resources, and a variety of other circumstances. The 1979 estimate of poverty for instance, provided no room for an individual's or a family's health care needs, since those were days when public delivery of health services was considered an entitlement. Today, with the reality of India's public health care system a large and growing scandal, there is a need to revisit that rather complacent assumption.

Recent policy decisions in the realm of education may have made a difference to the poor in terms of the access they have to publicly-funded institutions. The Supreme Court in 2002 decreed that government schools all over the country should introduce mid-day meals for all enrolled students with immediate effect. This directive has been implemented patchily, but surveys in states that were positive and responsive to this judicial decree, such as Rajasthan, have shown that school enrollment did indeed, increase as a consequence of the noon feedingprogramme.

Though educational access is not formally among the variables that goes into the poverty index, the derived impact on nutrition is something to be taken into account.

Noon feeding in schools relieves the typical family that lives on the margin of subsistence of the anxiety that a child sent to school any given day, might detract from economic earnings that particular day. Schooling for the poor is not about terms of years, but a day to day struggle. In terms of economic theory, the "opportunity cost" - i. e. , the earnings foregone - by sending children to school, even when education is free, is neutralised by the provision of noon meals.

The noon-meals programme also sets free the care-giver within the family - the mother or the older sister - to partake of economically earning activities and to supplement family earnings. While providing for better nutrition levels and reduced anxiety among female care-givers who are compelled to enter the labour market, noon feeding has contributed to poverty reduction in sparing the typical household the expense of providing one meal for its children. The rest of the family would conceivably enjoy better earnings and derivatively, improved access to nutrition and the other necessities of life, for the 180 days a year that the children are at school. The broader impact on poverty will have to wait one generation, when the children who gain an education today, grow to adulthood.

The poverty estimates that are available though, do not pertain to any moment in time when the noon feeding scheme may have had an impact for the better. Poverty is estimated on the basis of consumer expenditure surveys conducted by the National Sample Survey (NSS) Organisation every five years. The last available sample is from 2004 – 05 and all the arguments so far have revolved around this and two earlier surveys, of 1999 – 2000 and 1993 – 94.

A serious dissonance in the whole debate was introduced in the 1999 – 2000 round, which asked respondents about their consumption of certain of life's necessities and indulgences, over three distinct recall periods: one week, one month and one year. As experts pointed out then, this contaminated the data at source, rendering it incompatible with earlier estimations.

Simply for this reason, official claims thatIndia had made significant inroads in the battle against poverty in the years of liberalisation, proved contentious. In the official narration, poverty both in terms of ratio (i. e. , people living in poverty as a percentage of population) , as well as absolute number, had shown sharp declines between the consumer expenditure surveys undertaken in 1993 – 94, 1999 – 2000 and 2004 – 05. More serious scholars, who were by no means hostile to the programme of liberalisation, thought these claims rather overstretched. Certain among them, such as Angus Deaton of Princeton University, were prepared to concede that there had been a fall in the poverty ratio, though of not sufficient magnitude to make a dent in the absolute number of the poor. Others such as Abhijit Sen argued that the decade following 1995 had been a lost decade in the war against poverty, since the number of the poor had actually increased. [4]

The November 2009 expert group report, proposed a formula that would address the adequacy – or otherwise – of the poverty line measure as a representation of reality. Its inference was that if a broader definition were to be used, that took into account levels of not merely nutrition, but also other basic needs such as health, education and shelter, then the incidence of poverty is much greater than originally thought. And though there is no serious basis to question that the " comparable extent of poverty reduction" in the decades following liberalisation, is not dissimilar between the two methodologies, the claim that the number of the poor had declined did not quite pass muster. Indeed, there was, if anything, an increase in the number of the poor: from 403 million during the 1993 – 94 survey period, to 407 million during 2004 – 05. [5]

These figures still bear some good tidings, since they represent a decline in the poverty ratio. But for the Indian government, which has under fiscal pressure, been seeking to narrowly target its many social welfare commitments and confine them exclusively to the poor, this comes as unwelcome news. The intended savings on the fiscal front are unlikely tomaterialise, since there is no warrant in the poverty figures to cut budgetary subsidies in – for one thing – the distribution of foodgrain for the poor.

3

Fiscal difficulties and public welfare commitments

HowIndia sorts through these fiscal difficulties in the years to come, will be an important indicator of its commitment to making life more meaningful for well over a third of its citizens. Will India go by the *mantra* that growth rate is all that matters and that the poor will be adequately looked after in any high-growth regime? Or will it go back to the older wisdom that the poor hold the key to growth – that rather than depend on the fickle favours of "trickle-down", the greater assurance of economic development with justice and equality, lies in recognising the poor as the primary a-gents of the growth process.

From all that is available in the public realm, it seems clear that the government is backing growth as the antidote to poverty, rather than a direct attack on poverty as the pathway to growth. The official Economic Survey of the government of India, released every year just prior to the presentation of the Union Budget, sums up these philosophical dilemmas in its most recent edition, when it speaks of the improvement in human development index being "powered by per capita income growth" and then admits—rather implausibly and within the same paragraph – that India's "human development effort still needs to catch up with the capital".

There is an opinion that persistently surfaces in the daily referendum on the government that the media conducts: what is good for the economy is often bad for party politics. The economy in turn is assessed by the sole parameter of the aggregate level of growth. Parties often feel tempted to adopt fiscally irresponsible strategies when in power, especially when the electoral cycle is at a decisive moment. The media though has concluded that these efforts to abridge the natural course of economic growth and turn it to political advantage, serves little purpose. It only wrecks the opportunities for growth inherent inIndia's liberalisation drive.

The financial press and the news channels convinced themselves in 2004 thatIndia was "shining" when few others seemed inclined to that belief. And the party that had made "shining India" its claim for a renewed mandate to govern, went down to a momentous defeat in nation-wide general elections. It then became the accepted wisdom that despite the lustre that certain parts of India were displaying, a large part of the country remained in a slough of despond.

What could be done to restore the semblance of social and economic equity that a democratic polity depends upon? The government that took office in 2004, led by a party that had suffered a mortifying decade-long shutout from the corridors of power – when its self-belief in being the natural party of governance for all India was rudely shattered – saw the answer in revisiting the populist commitments of the 1970s and early-1980s. This meant providing a stimulus to the rural economy in an effort to directly address poverty, though within the overarching compulsions of fiscal prudence.

The National Rural Employment Guarantee Act (NREGA) was passed in 2005, assuring every willing individual a minimum of a hundred days of manual unskilled work, in the 200 poorest districts of the country. The fiscal year 2006 – 07 was the first full year of implementation of the National Rural Employment Guarantee Plan (soon named after Mahatma Gandhi and now known as the MNREGP).

RTI and the new regime of transparency

Theprogramme was in 2008 – 09 extended to the entire country at the urging of the Congress Party's youth leader, Rahul Gandhi. The four years in which the MN-REGP has been operative have also been professedly, an era of accountability in politics and transparency in bureaucratic functioning. This was the promise inherent in the Right to Information Act (RTI) that was among the first major legislative initiatives of the government that took office in 2004.

As with right to work legislation, RTI had been top priority for numerous civil society groups and left-wing political parties for at least a decade prior. But all campaign efforts had only succeeded in bringing forth a host of state – level laws, none of which had disclosure norms strong enough to be an effective tool of public accountability. The RTI law that was finally adopted by the Union Government in 2005 and given application over all ofIndia, was swiftly recognised as a truly ground-breaking law. There have since been numerous efforts to reassert bureaucratic privilege and whittle down some of its provisions. These have all been defeated by effective civil society mobilisation.

Because of the environment of information transparency in which it has been implemented, the MNREGP enjoys chances of success that were denied its predecessors. Indeed, the processes through which the MNREGP would function, particularly in relation to the public information function, the notification of beneficiaries, and payment of wages, were formulated by civil society actors who had been for years engaged in the RTI campaign, and had identified the precise vulnerabilities in earlier such welfareprogrammes. The MNREGP was in its basic design, programmed to avoid these pitfalls and to deliver maximum value to its intended beneficiaries.

A number of assessments of the MNREGP have been made in its first few years of operation, notably by the economist JeanDreze and his associates.[7] These have provided an encouraging early portrayal of the impact the programme has had on rural lives and livelihoods, and pointed to vital areas where improvements are necessary. Among the deficiencies, particularly noteworthy are the arbitrary process of fixing wages and the persistence of leakages through corruption. Again, though women have according to official data reviewed by Dreze, been between 40 and 44% of the beneficiaries of the MNREGP countrywide – and no less than 81% in the state of Tamil Nadu – the absence of childcare facilities has been identified as a serious impediment to more meaningful female participation.

Most of these failures as also all others, could be understood as arising from the evasion of bureaucratic accountability, which in turn is made possible by a collusive relationship between administrative staff and local power elites.

A formal evaluation of the MNREGP, conducted by an independent research institution on a mandate from the Planning Commission, has found a similarly mixed picture, with ample grounds for hope. A big worry from the perspective of this exercise, is the failure of the MNREGP to create embedded opportunities for work in the rural areas. Theprogramme has contributed to improved nutrition levels in the target areas. But it has not contributed in durable fashion to long-term work opportunities. This has in turn created two conditions, one of which – the failure to stem the tide of migration towards already choked urban India – is specifically identified as a concern.[8] In the interests of the long-term viability of the MNREGP, another implication needs to be taken into account: the purchasing power it has created has not been matched by an accummulation of productive assets in the rural areas.

This issue has not yet begun to crease brows within the Indian policy establishment, but it could soon begin to impinge on the viability of the rural jobs growth strategy. For long years sinceliberalisation kicked in as official policy, the Indian government refused to countenance any serious increase in rural welfare spending, simply because the priority was to reduce the budget deficit. The deficit was seen to be the principal cause of the twin evils of national indebtedness and rampant inflation.

There was a viewpoint articulated then, that fiscal investment in rural public worksprogrammes would not engender inflationary pressures, and that the budgetary pressures generated, would if at all, be minor and transient. All through the 1990s, buffer stocks of food with the government and its agencies were a veritable embarrassment of riches. Far in excess of prescribed norms, the carrying costs of these foodgrain stocks were beginning to seriously burden the public exchequer. An argument was advanced that in the circumstances, an increased outlays in rural public works, paid through the issue of foodgrain, would serve the welfare purpose of improving nutritional standards, while being consistent with fiscal pragmatism. Far from rising, the food subsidy bill would likely decline from an augmentation of rural public works programmes, since the enormous accretion of food stocks would be substantially drawn down. What was spent as a fiscal transfer to the rural poor would in other words, be more than made up by the savings effected in cutting the volume of food storage.

As with food, so also in several others sectors catering to the consumption demands of the poor, there was substantial excess capacity available in the economy through the 1990s. This in turn, led to realistic expectations that rising mass consumption demands, could easily be met by merely ramping up production, without the slightest risk of inflation.

5

Dealing with inflation

If the fiscal deficit was the reason why officialIndia resisted this seemingly irresist-ible demand, there were also warnings made from other quarters, less constrained by dogma, that the growth experience of the 1990s, continuing right till the early years of the 2000s, held quite a different message, with contrary welfare implications. It was a paradox of those years that an enormous accretion to food stocks with the gov-ernment occurred despite a steep decline in the growth rate of agriculture. The ex-cess of supply in other words, could have been achieved by suppressing the demand for food amongst the poor. Low growth rates in agriculture have been a feature of the years of liberalisation right till the current conjuncture. Yet these have also been a period of low inflation.

There is yet no credible economic theory that can explain the triple conjunction of declining per capita availability of essential food grain, rising inventories and low inflation in these mass consumption items. The low inflation experience of the years ofliberalisation seek another explanation, which may lie in the possibility of a harsh suppression of living standards at the lower end of the scale of income and wealth.

For ensuring its viability the rural jobsprogramme required that another serious complication in the labour market be attended to. A vast sea of unemployed workers was an assurance for agricultural capitalists who hired in farm labour, that the wages they paid would remain low. An employment guarantee would provide other options to the working population, forcing agricultural capitalist to hire in labour at likely higher wages. This would be transformed into a demand for higher support prices for the farm sector's surplus producers, creating a quite different dynamic in terms of the budget deficit, the prices at which food items are sold through the public distribution system and – through the exertions of the various pressure groups involved – a massive upward spiral of inflation.

Have these factors begun to work within the macro–economy of ruralIndia? The jury is still out on the question, though there is little doubt that inflation, especially in food and other mass consumption items, has begun to be a serious worry. The E-conomic Survey for 2009 – 10 speaks of "high double-digit food inflation" during the year, "especially in the second half", as a "major concern". Elsewhere, it attributes the rapid rise in prices of food items to "a deficient monsoon and expectations of shortage". [9]

Monsoon failure is a reflexive explanation for high food prices in a country where most crops are grown under rain – fed conditions and the majority depend for their livelihood on agriculture. In current circumstances, it is necessary to assess how credible this explanation is, by referring back to two recent years when rainfall deficiency was of a comparable magnitude.

In 2009, rainfall readings by the India Meteorological Department (IMD) put overall precipitation in the country at 77% of the long-period average. It is not quite easy to correlate rainfall deficiency with agricultural output and still less with inflation. But just to make the point abundantly clear, a comparison could be made with 2002, when country-wide rainfall was just 81% of the long-period average. Reaching back further, monsoon failure on a similar scale occurred last in 1987, when the national average was again, just 81% of the long-period average.

To take this comparison a little further, the official figure of inflation registered for the category "primary commodities" was 9. 7% in 1987 – 88 and 2. 6% in 2002 – 03. Addressing the theme of "Drought and Inflation", the *Economic Survey* for 2002 – 03 made the claim that: "In recent years, the agricultural economy has by and large moved from a shortage to a surplus situation and is thus more insulated against the vagaries of nature. Therefore, despite the failure of monsoon, average inflation rate remained low thanks to surplus stocks of foodgrains during the last three years". [10]

Yet, for 2009 – 10, the rate of inflation for "primary commodities" stood at 8. 8% , considerably above the figure for 2002 – 03 and very close to, though on the lower side, of the 1987 – 88 figure.

Sticklers for statistical accuracy may seek to explain these discrepancies in terms of four percentage points in rainfall – 81% versus 77% of long-term average – between 2009 and both the earlier years of comparison, i. e. , 2002 and 1987. The problem here is not just that the correlations are not one bit evident, but also that no relationship – even an approximate one – has been devised yet between rainfall deficiency, agricultural production and the behaviour of the market in grain.

Neither is the storage situation in grain a viable explanation for this seeming paradox, since the surplus – indeed the embarrassment of riches – has been a feature of the aftermath of the 2009 drought, as much, if not more so than before. Illustratively, the total volume of stock held by the Food Corporation of India (FCI) and other official agencies on July 1, 2003 – roughly a year after the monsoon failure of 2002 – was 35. 2 million tonnes. Comparing like for like, the total grain stock held by the same agencies on July 1, 2010, was 57. 8 million tonnes.

The recommended norm of stockholding for July 1 – which is a point in the agricultural cycle when growers all over India are preparing for their main sowing operations of the year – is 26. 9 milliontonnes. Since the world food price crisis of 2008, a "strategic reserve" of 2 million tonnes of rice and 3 million tonnes of wheat has been created in addition to this basic recommended stockholding. [11] All told, the volume of stocks held on July 1, 2009, was almost twice the recommended norm for that point in time. The reality that has come to light since then is that foodstocks are rotting for want of storage space. [12]

Figures, especially if they are drawn from arid official statistics, can never provide an adequate explanation for the multitude of real life situations and choices that farmers – who depend on local precipitation, soil quality, protective irrigation, and a complex of other factors – have to confront. But from merely looking at the inconsistencies between the official claims and the data put out in successive editions of the official *Economic Survey*, it becomes evident that the grandiose claim made in 2002 – 03, that the economy had been monsoon proofed, has proved rather hollow.

If the *Economic Survey* could characterise the post-monsoon scenario of 2002 as a "surplus situation", the same should apply to 2009, if anything with greater force. But if the "surplus" in 2003 was an adequate safeguard against inflation, an even greater surplus in 2010 is proving thoroughly inadequate. The *Economic Survey* in other words, is being reflexively lazy and intellectually dishonest in attributing the food inflation of 2010 to monsoon failure.

It can at this time only be offered as a hypothesis, but it needs to be inquired, if food price inflation is the consequence of the MNREGP unleashing long repressed consumption needs among the rural population. With the fiscal investment in rural employment yet to contribute substantively to asset productivity, this boost in purchasing power has not been matched by an increase in social product. And the wage employment opportunities afforded the rural poor through the MNREGP have increased bargaining power, allowing them to bid up the wages that the bigger farmers who hire inlabour would pay.

The figure below provides some indication of how rural development expenditures have moved over the last many years. Clearly, after the drought of 2002, the total outlay did not increase significantly, as it should have, if defending the purchasing power of the rural poor were at all a priority for the government of the day. In contrast, since the enactment of the MNREGA, the total budgetary commitment by both central and state governments in rural development has been stepped up a notch. It is an obvious inference then, that the MNREGP has fulfilled some part of its intended effect of creating greater purchasing power in the rural areas.

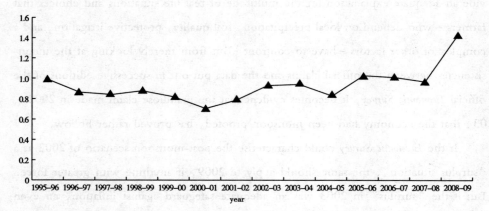

Total Rural Development Expenditure (Revenue and Capital) by Central and State Governments

Productive capacity though, may not quite be keeping pace, which means that the inflationary genie, bottled up through the early years ofliberalisation, is now unfettered. If past is prologue, then the official response to this inflationary threat would most likely target the budget allocated in rural public works programmes for the first cut.

The Food and Agricultural Organisation (FAO) has found that successful strategies to cope with poverty and undernourishment have invariably involved a high rate of growth in agriculture, increasing per capita food availability and significant official spending on public health. [13] None of these conditions has been met in India since the onset of liberalisation. Indeed, the record has if anything, been the reverse.

So where doesIndia's confidence that it is making substantive progress in the battle against poverty come from? There is no official explanation forthcoming – for obvious reasons – on what underlies the new mood of sunny optimism in the Indian policy establishment. Official spokespersons though are quick to question contrary information, even as they ignore inconvenient findings. Undeniably though, the most important contribution to the brash new mood, has been India's own growth record over the two decades of liberalisation. And if the first decade was ambiguous in terms of its outcome, the second has tended with seeming lack of equivocation, to underline the message of a "shining India".

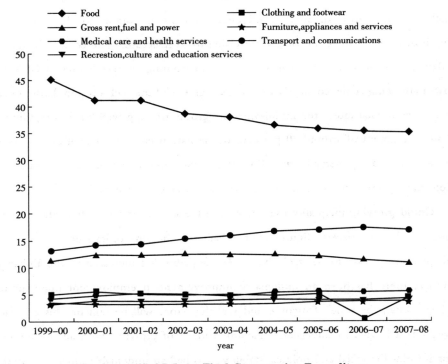

Components of Private Final Consumption Expenditure

If the sources of growth were to beanalysed, it would become apparent that the principal impetus has come from an increase in capital formation rates. Total consumption expenditure has declined as a percentage of GDP. Government's consumption expenditure has stayed at a relatively high proportion of GDP, and private final consumption expenditure (PFCE) has shown important compositional shifts, with the traditional staples of subsistence – food, clothing and shelter – cumulatively show-

ing a sharp fall in relation to the total. The growing segments of private final consumption indeed are those of special interest to the upper and middle strata, such as
transportation equipment, communication, health care services and recreational, cul-
tural and education services.

This particular pattern of growth is to be viewed in the context of the increase
in income and wealth inequality in the Indian economy. [14] The two indeed are inti-
mately linked. This is an obvious inference from the age-old verity that the rate of
growth of an economy is inevitably correlated to its structure. The economist Kaushik Basu puts it thus in a recent paper: "The outstanding average figures of GDP and
growth are being achieved largely by a small segment of the well-off population growing at phenomenal rates, the middle-income group growing well but less rapidly and
a bottom segment of around 20 per cent of the nation growing at snail's pace. What
this suggests about poverty is true. Poverty, as measured by the percentage of people
below the poverty line is declining but at a rate that is unacceptably low". [15]

Could growing inequality itself be part of the key to understanding the relatively
modest decline in poverty figures sinceglobalisation became official policy? There is
perhaps a strong case to be made here. As inequality has increased in the Indian e-
conomy, there has been an undeniable improvement in employment opportunities
trickling down the scale of income and wealth. More will be said on this at a later
stage, but it is vital to understand that this pattern of growth, with all the implications it holds for social and political stability, has had an undeniable impact on India's
evolving relationship with the global community.

One implication has been a reluctance to stand up for the values of equity and
fairness in global councils, since the enforcement of these norms – as for instance the
demand for transparency in global capital flows – could in the short term, damage
India's growth prospects. A second has been the export of the "every man for him-
self" attitude to the country's moral and political engagement with the global community. India's leadership of the developing world in most key global negotiations, now

comes qualified by its ambition to be not merely first among equals, but unquestioned hegemon.

This change in attitude shows up in most engagements thatIndia has undertaken in world affairs, but most so in neighbourhood affairs. There is frequently an argument advanced within the country, that India should forget about its global ambitions and engage within the neighbourhood in a constructive manner, with honest intent to put behind the numerous burdens that its unique history has imposed. This line of thinking is a minimal strain within the mainstream of the "shining India" doctrine.

6

First steps for meaningful and credible global engagement

India has been in recent times, increasingly active as a player in global pressure groups such as IBSA, BASIC and BRIC. These have helped cement a common position within multilateral forums that puts developed country interests first and limits the susceptibility of each to the pressures that industrialised countries are known to exert, often leveraging bilateral trade and donor relationships to ensure that opposing views are banished from the negotiating table. The foundation for these groupings was perhaps laid in the build-up to the fifth ministerial conference of the World Trade Organisation (WTO) in Cancun, Mexico, in September 2003. Confronted with the familiar spectacle of the industrialised countries seeking to run away with the ball by putting out pre – conference statements and proposals that reflected their exclusive concerns, India, Brazil and South Africa came together to draw up a detailed and specific list of conditions that the U. S. and the E. U. needed to fulfil in the agricultural realm, if the global trade talks were to make any meaningful progress. [16]

The coalition held firm at the Cancun trade summit that followed and indeed, drew in a number of other countries with strong interests in terms both of protecting vulnerable smallholding peasants at home and capturing agricultural export markets.

Inherent differences between Brazil, South Africa and India – not to mention Thailand, Argentina and other countries that made common cause at Cancun – made the coalition an unstable one, prone to fracture at the slightest hint of a concession to its minimum bargaining position. Yet, the obduracy of the U. S. and the E. U. on agricultural subsidies proved a powerful adhesive. The coalition of India, Brazil and South Africa came through that encounter with greatly enhanced image and credibility.

The team has since gone forward to expand its range and sharpen its focus. IBSA is now a grouping that articulates far-reaching positions of consequence to the developing world at a number of global forums. It has also become a quasi-formal political grouping with regular summit meetings at which issues of mutual interest are discussed. At its most recent summit in the Brazilian capital, IBSA agreed to jointly develop a satellite and to closely coordinate national positions on a range of issues, such as U. N. reform, climate change and the world trade negotiations.

Another grouping with quite different scope and focus emerged quite fortuitously from a far – fetched forecast by an economist in the Goldman Sachs brokerage firm in 2001. The forecast that four nations – Brazil, Russia, India and China – between them accounting for 40% of the global population and a quarter of the land area, would by 2050 be the dominant economies, supplanting all the powers of the day, proved to be irresistibly attractive. And it came at a time when countries that had been mute spectators to the unilateralist rampage of the U. S. , intent on invading a country on false pretexts, were beginning to articulate their deep misgivings.

Soon after the U. S. invasion of Iraq, the Shanghai Five – a grouping promoted by Russia, China and three former Soviet republics from Central Asia, in the wake of the Taliban takeover of Afghanistan in 1996 – was expanded to bring in Uzbekistan, and formally given the title of the Shanghai Cooperation Organisation (SCO). Though India remained tepid to begin with, in part because of the SCO's barely concealed strategic purpose of checking U. S. hegemonic power, it has since (in

2005) signed up as an observer, to ensure that its concerns in regard to Afghanistan and Pakistan gain reasonable traction.

BRIC involved a bit of the SCO and a bit of IBSA coalescing around a nucleus of shared objectives, which have not proved very easy to identify or define. This has especially been the case sinceIndia has been cast – in its new strategic partnership with the U. S. – as a countervailing force to China's growing regional and global influence. But in large part as a consequence of Russian initiatives, discussions among the four BRIC nations began in 2006 towards forming a formal grouping, culminating in the first official summit of the four in Ekaterinburg, Russia in 2009.

A 16-point statement adopted at the end of the summit spoke of the reform of international financial institutions as a high priority item for a more stable global order. It spoke of the imperative need to enhance the voice of the transition economies and the developing countries in the constitution of the top management councils of these institutions. And in a barely concealed reference to theunviability of continuing with the U. S. dollar as *de facto* world reserve currency, it called for a "stable, predictable and more diversified international monetary system. "[17]

Given the complexity of global issues thatIndia faces, a bit of BRIC soon attached itself to IBSA, with China teaming up with that three member grouping to constitute yet another ingredient in the teeming alphabet soup of regional and inter – regional groupings, this one referred to as BASIC.

All three groupings were in play in April inBrasilia when IBSA first conducted its deliberations and drew up an agenda for future action in the realm of development. This was followed immediately afterwards, by BRIC which expatiated upon its concerns on the global economic order. And then was the turn of BASIC. South Africa came back into the meeting room while Russia packed its bags and left, to make space for China as the player that matters in the global dialogue on climate change.

Achieving coherence between multiple forums

India has a clearly stated interest in keeping these forums distinct from each other. It has styled IBSA as the democratic forum where an inter-continental grouping speaks for a wider constituency. The hidden sub-text here is clearly that the three democracies, each with a claim to speak for its wider continent, would have greater credibility in any direct engagement with the western powers that largely dictate global economic affairs. India is also unconvinced that BRIC would be a suitable vehicle for its larger geopolitical ambitions, simply because of the presence of China. Though the 16-point statement adopted at the first BRIC summit did make the appropriate noises about U. N. reform and ceremonially bow towards India's ambitions to be seated at the high table, it stopped short of explicitly endorsing India's case for permanent membership in the U. N. Security Council. China evidently believes that a permanent berth is not something that can be granted as long as India has unfinished business with itself and Pakistan.

When asked after the April conclaves if this multiplicity of inter-regional groupings could operate with enhanced efficacy if some were to write themselves out of business and the others were to define clear membership norms, Indian Prime Minister Manmohan Singh was quite categorical about the need for each to maintain a separate existence: "IBSA has a personality of its own. It is three separate continents, three democracies. BRIC is a conception devised by Goldman Sachs. We are trying to put life into it". [18]

What purpose though is being sought through these multiple forums? The WTO has receded from public attention since theHong Kong ministerial meeting produced an agreement that was the most modest of all time in terms of ambition, since it stayed deliberately clear of every member country's deepest sensitivities. Since then, the WTO has missed one biennial deadline to hold a ministerial conference, its highest deliberative forum and seemingly roused itself into holding one in its head-quarters city of Geneva in December 2009, only in order to be in formal compliance with an important commitment to its membership. It was made clear then that the conference would not be a negotiating forum, but merely an occasion to review pro-gress and reaffirm faltering commitments.

In September 2009, India hosted a meeting of the WTO's heavy-hitters, in a signal of solidarity with the aims of free trade as also a symbolic gesture of the develo-ping countries' willingness to assert their status as stakeholders in the multilateral trade negotiations.

Expectedly, the WTO talks have made little progress since proposals drawn up in July 2008 in the three most contentious areas of agriculture, non-agricultural mar-ket access (NAMA, or industrial tariffs, in simpler language) and services, led to a sputtering start to the negotiations over a year later. It has been an arduous process getting the balance right in a negotiating process where nothing is agreed until every-thing is. The industrialised countries are tenacious in holding out on subsidies and other measures of support for agriculture, while India and the developing world are ruling out any further tariff cuts on industrial goods till substantive progress is achieved in improving agricultural market access. As long as the stalemate persists – and the chances now are that it will, since the global economic recession has energised pro-tectionist voices – the unity of the IBSA forum will hold. Unless, that is, any one member chooses to strike a deal on the side.

The proposals on agriculture submitted byIndia and other countries at Cancun, were remarkable in seeking to harmonise the interests of developing country exporters and large peasant economies that have a strong defensive interest in protecting their markets. India counted itself quite decisively in the second category, whereas Brazil unequivocally was in the first. The common element that bonded the two and brought South Africa in as a player on the same team, was the relatively diversified industrial base that these countries have built up, which endows them with a strong interest in holding out on the NAMA negotiations till they get what they want in agriculture. That the unity forged in Cancun has, despite a potential divergence, lasted right till the Hong Kong conference and beyond, speaks of a determination to ensure that the errors of the Uruguay Round are not repeated.

Expectedly, very little came out of the September 2009 mini-ministerial inDelhi. The most recent news – flash from the WTO is that eleven panels have been set up with five countries (or trading blocs) participating, to consider how to cut through the logjam, particularly in relation to the three areas of agriculture, NAMA and services trade. India is one of the five, along with the E. U. , the U. S. , Brazil and China. [19] India's alliance with Brazil within the WTO arena will be tested in this round of bargaining, though China's presence adds an imponderable.

India and other developing countries forced agriculture onto the multilateral trade agenda during the Uruguay round of negotiations, as part of a deal which included the dismantlement of quotas in the textile trade and the enactment of new rules on intellectual property rights. Concessions rendered by the industrialised countries on agriculture have remained illusory at best. Gains in this sector have been slender to the developing countries in general, and negligible to India in particular.

Far from flourishing in the new environment of global trade, Indian agriculture in the years since the Uruguay Round agreements came into effect, has fallen into a slough of despond. Appropriately enough for a body with intrusive jurisdiction over diverse economic activities, the WTO came to be a natural focus for livelihood anxieties and grievances in a time of great uncertainty for agriculture. Over the first decade of its existence, the WTO was ascribed with direct responsibility for the crisis of livelihoods in agrarianIndia.

This story is not heard with quite the same stridency any more, since the prolonged negotiating stalemate has seen the WTO receding from public attention. But even in the glory days of the WTO, the story was, as with all others that originate in the realm of demonology, highly overdrawn. The WTO did of course have the potential to bite deep into the material well – being of the Indian agricultural sector, but its main impact still remains to be played out. Following prolonged and often acrimonious negotiations with major trading blocs under WTO auspices, India agreed early in 2000 to phase out all quantitative restrictions (QRs) on imports on an accelerated schedule. With effect from April 1, 2001, India had no QRs operating in its foreign trade, only protective duties.

The dismantling of QRs came with an explicit assurance that India would retain flexibility by way of tariffs to offset any unsettling surge in farm sector imports. India has so far managed to keep its "bound" tariffs – the maximum duties it can charge – at among the highest within the WTO membership. So there is little substance in the argument that the WTO disciplines have been responsible for the crisis in Indian agriculture.

Going beyond the emotional rhetoric about the WTO, the most cursory examination of the disciplines it imposes would show thatIndia is well within the envelope in fulfilling its obligations. An exercise done when the WTO negotiations were reaching a decisive stage in the mid-1990s, found that India's agricultural subsidies were firmly in negative territory, i. e., with international price levels as the datum, Indian agriculture in the aggregate was taxed rather than subsidised. [20] There is no basis to believe since then, that the picture has changed in any significant respect.

The troubled state of Indian agriculture in short, is entirely a home-grown creation, born in years of under-investment and in particular, a shocking retreat of the public sector from its role as the agency that creates the enabling conditions and incentives for private sector commitment to productivity augmentation. With occupational diversification inIndia being an extremely slow process and over half the country still dependent on agriculture for livelihood, inter-generational fragmentation of land-holdings is rapidly eroding the viability of individual farms. This makes the active involvement of public agencies in the creation of overhead capital especially vital, if productivity improvements are to be sustained. This however, has been an area of continuing default by the Indian state.

Second wind for the Indian growth process

It is accepted by wide consensus that the Indian economy acquired a second wind in 2003 – 04 and moved to a new trajectory of near double-digit growth. [21] There is also general agreement that one of the most significant contributions to the new growth momentum came from the rise in gross domestic savings. After being in negative territory for years together, public sector saving turned positive in 2003 – 04 and has since continued to increase strongly. Also turning in a strong performance in the early part of the decade was private corporate saving, which increased from between 3. 75 and 4. 75 percent of GDP in the first four years, to over 7 per cent in 2004 – 05 and all subsequent years. The year 2008 – 09 brought about a partial reversal of both these trends, since private corporate sector earnings were deeply eroded by the global economic downturn, and the compulsion of fighting the recession through a fiscal stimulus obliged the public sector to undertake a number of fresh expenditure commitments. Household savings also increased in the years beginning in 2003, though after a relative lag in relation to the public sector and private corporate sector.

The public sector began to boost its total savings after the enactment of the Fiscal Responsibility and Budget Management Act of 2001. From the financial year 2002 –

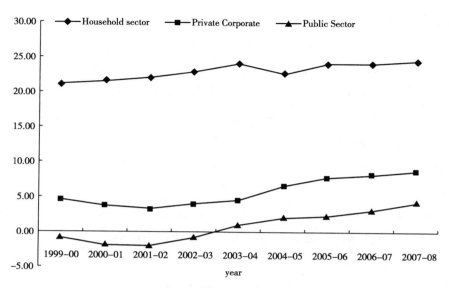

Savings by Sector as % of GDP

03, there has been an effort to restrain the growth of expenditure, that has fetched results in the following years. And to silence the critics, the burden of adjustment has been borne in the main by what are classified as the "non – developmental expenditures" of central and state governments. [22] The softening of interest rates, which led to smaller debt servicing obligations on accummulated public sector borrowings, had a role to play here, as did the relative moderation in the growth of the defence budget over the relevant years.

On the other side of the story, revenue receipts of both the central and state governments grew rapidly through these years. As a percentage of GDP, tax receipts at these two tiers of the government showed signs of regaining the levels they were at, prior to the inauguration of the economic reforms in 1991.

There are few comprehensive studies of the growth of private sector profitability in the first decade of the 2000s. But evidence points to robust growth in sales and good earnings under the head "other income", [23] suggesting good returns on corporate investments in shares through this period of a virtually uninterrupted bull run in the country's stockmarkets.

Another notable change occurred in the country's growth profile in this period: the growing interest of foreign investors. After a decade-and-a-half of fairly indifferent or only sporadic interest in the Indian market – as a destination for both direct and portfolio investment – foreign capital began flowing in to Indian stockmarkets in significant magnitudes from about 2003 – 04. Direct investment though, remained modest even through these years, but registered sharp upticks in 2007 – 08 and the following year.

Portfolio investments though large in volume, have remained volatile, with large inflows typically being accompanied by large withdrawals. Thus after registering

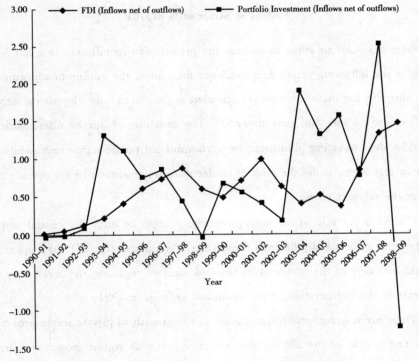

FDI (Inflows net of outflows) Portfolio Investment (Inflows net of outflows)

a historic high of 2. 52% of GDP in 2007 – 08 , net portfolio investments (i. e. , in-flows less outflows) fell to a negative figure the following year as investors pulled out in the wake of the global economic meltdown, to put their money into shoring up falteringstockmarkets in their home countries.

What is classified as FDI too is a very ambiguous entity. Research by the econo-mist Chalapati Rao indicates that over half the inflow of FDI in the period of interest originated in known tax havens, especially Mauritius. A large part of the inflow was for acquisition of shares in existing companies and cannot be deemed to have added to productive capacity. And over 70% of the inflow was in the services sector – no-tably real estate and construction and financial services – as against just over 20% in manufacturing. [24]

As interesting as the Indian growth story since 2003 – 04 – perhaps more so if the connection between the two were to be drawn out – has been the huge apprecia-tion in asset prices since then. Stock values for instance, multiplied manifold. Taking just the one indicator of the market capitalisation on the Bombay Stock Exchange, i. e. , the total value of shares listed on this most active of India's bourses, went up from just over 23% of GDP in 2002 – 03 to over 100% in 2007 – 08. [25] The follow-ing year, the figure collapsed though it was still many times higher than before the es-calation began.

Anecdotally, note could be taken of similar trends in the real estate market too. The absence of a reliable index of real estate values makes a definitive assessment of this phenomenon difficult. [26] From RBI data, though, we do know that bank ad-vances for house purchases increased vastly in the years under consideration. "Personal loans" were the fastest growing component of overall bank credit in the period 2000 – 01 to 2006 – 07. And of these, housing loans had by far the largest share.

Bank credit, liberally extended, could have fuelled the speculative rise in house prices in this period of high economic growth. Official explanations put the rise in prices down to the growth in disposable incomes attendant on high income accruals to

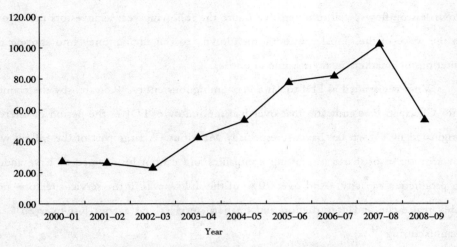

Growth in Stockmarket Capitalisation (BSE Index)

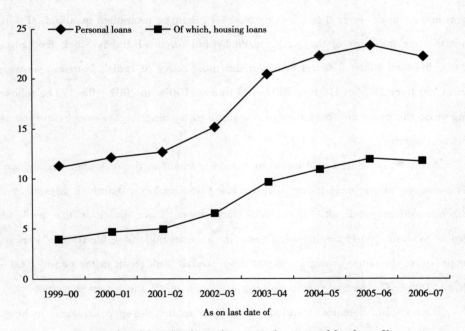

Personal and housing loans in proportion to total bank credit

those professionally employed in the major cities. This in itself does not constitute a sufficient explanation, since it does not offer any estimate of how far current incomes within the professional upwardly mobile sections benefited from the acceleration of growth rates. It also fails to address the key determinant of the banking sector and its role in aggressively pursuing a line of business opened up in the new environment ofliberalisation, and financing multiple home purchases by the upwardly mobile professional classes.

Another aspect of the asset price boom of the years between 2003 and 2008 needs to be taken note of. This was a period of easy credit availability, low interest rates and high liquidity in the economy. Conditions that could have resulted in a commodity price inflation contributed instead, to an asset price inflation. This rise in asset prices beyond what the "fundamentals" may warrant, could contribute in the short-term to ecoonomic growth by providing a stimulus to personal consumption by asset holders. In conditions of high liquidity, banks and financial institutions are often willing to refinance asset purchases, allowing the asset owner to cash in on the growth of his ownership equity. [27] Very little work has been done towards identifying the role played by this so-called "wealth effect" in the recent Indian growth story. But it is a feasible hypothesis that such a contribution has indeed been made. In that case, a reverse wealth effect should be anticipated when asset values start contracting and credit institutions start providing for bad advances made against fickle asset values. By the same criterion, the slide in property values could affect bank solvency seriously if it continues for much longer.

Following a year of serious worry, capital inflow into the Indian economy revived in 2009 – 10. As with all such matters, there is no clear or coherent explanation available, except that international investors after the phase of panic when they were repatriating capital home to defend against inclement winds, are now in a frame of mind to venture forth again. And the story runs, India occupies prime position among the overseas destinations that investors have regained interest in, on account of its immense growth prospects. Since that explanation was advanced in the Economic Survey for 2009 – 10 – released in February 2010 – things have changed dramatically. The following prognosis of the Economic Survey now seems decidedly askew: ".. there are signs of recovery in the global economy with the U. S. , Euro Zone and Japan already out of recession and the momentum of growth picking up in emerging economies".[28] Since it was made, there have been contrary developments in the Euro Zone, the U. S. , as well as Japan.

Greece plunged into a deficit induced crisis that put Euro-zone unity and monetary coherence in jeopardy, prompting a bailout of record magnitude, pushed through in the teeth of immense resistance from the lower and middle-income groups. The U. S. has registered several successive months of aggregate economy-wide job losses[29] and political discord over the fiscal commitments that the Barack Obama administration has made to lift the economy out of recession, is plunging the country towards policy gridlock and potentially, the most counter-productive response possible in a crisis situation. Japan went through a wrenching political change, forcing out of office a Prime Minister installed with expectations that he would pull the economy out of its two-decade long slump. But his successor is under challenge from within the ruling party and the appreciation of the Japanese yen, seen as a necessary ingredient for global recovery in both the U. S. and the Euro-zone, is viewed quite unequivocally as the source of all misfortune in Japan.

What is the policy response that would be best designed to pull the global economy out of recession? The reality is that very few answers are available, whether easy or otherwise. What seems the most logical course of action for the U. S. , is seen to be deeply damaging by the Euro Zone and Japan. If the U. S. and the Euro Zone are convinced that Japan bears principal responsibility to pump up its economy and bring in much needed vigour into the global recovery, Japan itself sees that it is being made to bear a disproportionate burden for remedying a situation brought into existence by U. S. profligacy and the subtle mechanisms of protectionism that the Euro

Zone has put in place.

Discord between the heavy-hitters is running high and smaller players are unlikely to get much of an audience for any opinion they may have on what it would take to get the global economy moving. After years of confining the discussion within the rich club – first the G-7 and then in recognition of the strategic clout that Russia brought to the table, expanding it to the G-8 – global power brokers have now conceded that other stakeholders too need to be given a place in the privileged conference halls if there is to be meaningful progress towards setting right the grievous imbalances in the world economy. The G-8 retains its separate existence, but every summit now is conjoined with the broader deliberations of the G-20, at which India, Brazil, South Africa and a number of other countries are heard.

9

The G-20 Forum and its Potentialities

For the record, at the last summit of the G-20 in Toronto, Canada in June 2010, India opposed the proposal to tax speculative capital flows that have been causing undue volatility in developing countries.

This is consistent with domestic tax policy inIndia, where capital gains earned in the stockmarket go untaxed, as too do dividends earned from equity ownership. India's posture on a global policy issue of concern in these times of capital volatility, is defensive of its short-term interests and hamstrung by its own recent growth record, which is perhaps highly dependent on short-term capital inflows and fleeting upticks in asset values that create an illusion of durable wealth creation. Without having ever ventured to institute any substantive taxes on speculative capital flows, India's policy establishment has learnt the hard way that verbal concessions to the need of such a levy, are likely to be severely punished by global investors. [30] With India's growth record now seen to be in a precarious state, official spokesmen are likely to be extra cautious in terms of the options they are seen to be considering.

India's official posture towards the G-20 is, judging by the tone of the commentary offered in the most recent Economic Survey, highly positive. This is a forum that has become more active than before, ramping up its annual gatherings from one to two in 2009 and resolving to do likewise in 2010. The Toronto summit of June will be followed in November by one in Seoul.

The G-20, has according to the Economic Survey for 2009 – 10, agreed among itself, that it will be "the premier forum for international economic cooperation".

Intentions aside, it needs to be asked if the G-20 has the internal coherence to provide the clear-sighted leadership the world needs at this time. The deafening political discord that the

U. S. – still the singular fulcrum of the global economy – is experiencing, does not carry the faintest suggestion that it can show the breadth of vision to carry the rest of the world forward in concerted action to remedy collective economic ills.

On December 31, 2010, the massive tax concessions introduced by the George Bush administration in 2001 are due to expire. That they were introduced just as the U. S. was entering into international military engagements that called for greater resource mobilisation efforts, showed that the tax cuts were ill-conceived to begin with. A so-called "sunset clause" on the tax cuts was an opportunistic compromise between the opposition Democrats and Bush's Republican party, since none among them was really sure where the measure – the quintessential triumph of ideology over commonsense – was taking the country.

As PresidentBarack Obama nears his moment of decision on whether to retain the Bush tax cuts or not, he is besieged by the Tea Party movement which has likened the slightest retreat to a form of treason. Obama's instinct, consistent with the advice of all but the fiscal fantasists, is to do away with the tax cuts for the upper – income groups, i. e. , those earning in excess of a quarter-million dollars a year, and to stimulate the economy by cutting taxes for the lower and middle-income groups.

Prescriptions for the current paralysis of the world economy, devised by well-regarded and socially responsible economists, provide an indication of how deep the policy dilemmas are. Raghuraman G. Rajan of Chicago University – a former chief economist of the IMF – believes that the U. S. would have to cut its deficit by slashing expenditure and if necessary, raising taxes selectively. He also insists that the Chinese and Japanese governments, which hold enormous accummulations of dollar bonds, should revalue their currencies.

These are themes that have been sounded at various times over the last many years, without ever eliciting the cooperative responses required. The reasons are fairly clear. In the mid-1980s, the U. S. economy was about to suffer seizure on account of the value of the dollar, then ruling at record highs, despite chronic and growing trade deficits. The deficits in turn, were a direct consequence of the voodoo economics introduced by the hugely revered Ronald Reagan, who cut taxes, raised defence spending and promised that he would balance the budget at the same time. There was obviously no way that this circle could be squared. But the external account deficits that the U. S. economy then began to run, proved limitlessly expandable, simply because the U. S. dollar was the world reserve currency.

As chief economist of the IMF, Rajan was at the centre of an effort in 2006 to bring the five economies that had the greatest stake in remedying the growing global imabalances to some semblance of concord on the best strategy available. The U. S. , the E. U. , China, Japan and Saudi Arabia were involved in this round of extensive consultations under the aegis of the IMF. The upshot as described by Rajan is worth reproducing in his own words: "The response from our interlocutors was .. pretty uniform. Countries agreed that the trade imbalances were a potential source of instability and economic reforms were needed to bring them down before markets took fright or politicians decided to enter the fray with protectionist measures. But each country was then quick to point out why it was not responsible for the imbalances and why it would be so much easier for some other country to push a magic button to make them disappear". [31]

Rajan abandoned the effort and returned to his university job a dejected man.

When the consultations had run their course, the IMF put out an anodyne statement claiming success: they talks, said the IMF, had provided room for a "free and frank exchange of views". As Rajan acidly notes, this is little else than diplomatic-speak for "total disagreement".

The U. S. sees its external debt as a consequence of excessive savings in China and Japan – and various other countries – and their willingness to build up an infinite store of U. S. treasury bonds. In this reading, the principal onus for correcting the global imbalances rests on China, which has for far too long, pegged its currency at a value far below what fundamentals would dictate.

On the other side of the fence, China sees the U. S. consumption binge of the last two decades as the principal cause of global imbalances. It denies that its currency policies have anything to do with the problem and insists that it will follow its own gradualist path in realigning the Chinese yuan with other major world currencies. China also points out that if it were to revalue its currency to appease U. S. sensibilities it could well fall into the kind of long-term economic paralysis that Japan has suffered since 1986, when it relented under insistent pressure and adjusted the yen value upwards against the U. S. dollar.

Changing demographics will also play a role in the years ahead. China's demographic "dependency ratio" – i. e. , the ratio of the population below 14 and above 65, to the population between these ages – has been rapidly falling but will bottom out in 2010 and increase in the years ahead. This has obvious implications for its savings rate and could induce it to prioritise current savings rather than consumption in preparation for the likely demographic scenario of the 2020s, when it would have a larger dependent population to care for.

Adjusting currency values upwards will also have to be assessed as an option, against the compulsion that the world's surplus economies face, of sustaining the value of their holdings of U. S. government bonds. And if the bonds were to decline in value, the U. S. would have to raise interest rates to keep the world interested in fi-

nancing its still unbridged deficit. That in turn would cause immense distress in an e-
conomy steeped at all levels in debt.

The Nobel laureate economist PaulKrugman is among the most vocal in calling
on China for credible currency reforms. But in terms of the antidote for the U. S.
economy's current ills, his prescription runs along conventional Keynesian lines:
stepped up public spending financed in part by fresh taxes and an interventionist Federal Reserve that would buy up debt instruments such as mortgage backed securities
to inject much needed purchasing power into the economy. [32] How far such a strategy would be consistent with the depreciation of the U. S. dollar's value against other
major world currencies, is a matter that he does not go into. But the credibility of
the U. S. dollar and the sustenance of its value are of obvious importance if the
Keynesian strategy is to stand even a halfway chance of success.

As Rajan records, policymakers in China are dismissive of accusations that they
manipulate currency values and see them as a very lame alibi for the failures of U. S.
economic competitiveness. The scenario as they see it, is simply that if Chinese exports were taken out of the equation by an appreciation of the yuan against the
dollar, their place would be taken by Cambodian and Vietnamese exports. The
U. S. deficit would remain a constant in all scenarios. Only the countries that run
the counterpart surpluses would change.

There is undoubtedly a point here, since the U. S. began life as a deficit economy in the 1980s when the counterpart surpluses were run by Japan, the oil exporting
states of the Gulf and Germany (or West Germany as it then was). German unifica-
tion took West Germany out of this equation and the appreciation of the yen beginning in 1986 and the opening up of major Japanese manufacturing locations in the
U. S., mitigated some of Japan's bilateral imbalances. But the U. S. deficit continued to soar, with China, certain Latin American states and several East and South-
East Asian countries clocking up the counterpart surpluses.

The U. S. dilemma is deepseated and structural. And like all such malaises, it calls for structural remedies. Mere cosmetic changes to exchange rates can do little to redress the loss of U. S. manufacturing competitiveness, which has been evident since the 1960s but became an irreversible fact with financial services literally taking over the economy in the Reagan years.

10

The challenge of climate change and India's response

Economic growth is driven by inanimate sources of energy and developing countries, as they embark on the pathway towards securing standards of living comparable to the west, face irksome constraints from the depletion of the global environmental commons. If all countries were to go about their economic growth strategies in the "business as usual" mode, planet earth could soon sink rapidly towards the catastrophe of irreversible climate change.

Climate change is a global challenge that nations are called upon to confront with a common sense of purpose, without allowing nationalist ideologies and transient advantages on the geopolitical checkerboard to detract from longer-term goal. But this is precisely where inflexible national interests have most obtrusively come into play, causing bitter acrimony in all global negotiating forums.

Equity demands that theindustrialised countries which together bear direct responsibility for an estimated 80% of the accummulation of greenhouse gases (GHGs), should bear a proportionate share of the burden of averting the looming environmental catastrophe. At the same time, the industrialised countries have the responsibility of evolving an alternative to the highly carbon-intensive developmental

paradigm that they have adopted and to make the underlying technologies and processes available in an affordable format to the developing world.

Industrialised countries (IC's), with a few exceptions such as Germany and the
U. K. , have resisted this common sense with an obduracy that has brought global climate change negotiations to a virtual standstill. IC's continue to be in default on their
obligations to cut GHG emissions, as agreed under the Kyoto protocol of 1992. E-
ven the commitment to partly offset IC emissions by developing and funding mitiga-
tion strategies in developing countries, remains unmet in most part.

Kyoto was a partially successful agreement in that it imposed binding obligations
on all the countries that have contributed to looming environmental catastrophe. It
also enshrined the principle of "common and differentiated responsibilities" in ac-
cordance with the unmet developmental aspirations of particular countries and the historic role of the IC's in the atmospheric buildup of GHGs. But in making the shrink-
ing space of the global environmental commons a tradeable commodity that could be
bought and sold – typically in a manner that would suit the compulsions of the industrialised countries – Kyoto set a very poor example for future negotiations.

A review of how farindustrialised countries had met emissions reduction targets,
conducted just prior to the Copenhagen climate summit in December 2009, revealed
serious defaults by virtually all. Yet the negotiations at Copenhagen failed to show
any seriousness of intent and the yawning trust deficit between the IC's and the developing world was if anything, enhanced by the procedures adopted. The declaration
that finally emerged had nothing more substantive than an affirmation that the world's
poorest countries deserved added financial support to face the imminent challenges of
climate change. This was regarded, rightly, as a betrayal of the mandate that the
conference opened with, since the IC's were expected at Copenhagen, to accept a
measure of responsibility commensurate with their historic role in creating the atmospheric burden of GHGs.

India was among the countries press-ganged into a last minute compromise which proved a figleaf too paltry to cover the evidence of gross failure. Since Copenhagen, India has shown some signals that it is willing to move beyond its insistence that the developing countries' obligations will begin to kick in only when the industrialised world has fulfilled its side of the bargain.

Policy circles inIndia are awakening now to the fact that the absolute volume of carbon emissions the country puts into the atmosphere is substantial. Though modest on a *per capita* basis, it is still a considerable addition to the GHG burden at a time when scientific research has found that the earlier target of reducing carbon concentration to 450 parts per million by volume (ppmv) by 2020 is over – generous. Though yet to be accepted within official multilateral forums, the call for a reduction to 350 ppmv by 2020 – made by James Hansen, who has reasonable claims to being the world's most respected climate scientist – cannot be ignored.

The only firm quantitative commitment thatIndia has made is in terms of *per capita* emissions. Prime Minister Manmohan Singh has reportedly assured German Chancellor Angela Merkel that India's *per capita* emissions will never exceed IC levels. This remains a covenant of uncertain validity and enforceability, but calculations by the Delhi Science Forum, an independent policy research group, have shown that if India were to follow a "business as usual scenario" and the western countries were to live upto commitments on emissions reduction, then India could well exceed the industrialised world in terms of *per capita* emissions at a not too distant point in the future. [33]

A strategic choice is clearly called for. Continuing insistence on the norm of equity and "shared and differentiated responsibility", will mean that the IC's will continue to use India's inaction as an alibi for their own. India's strategy in turn is seen as one of "hiding behind the skirt of western inaction" [34]. The two in conjunction have become a recipe for a complete paralysis of the global negotiations.

India's newfound awareness that it has to initiate credible action on its own, comes even as several developing countries and small island nations show increasing signs of restiveness at the stalemate. The matter is especially important for South A-sia, which lives in the shadow of the Himalayas and has two countries, Bangladesh and the Maldives, that suffer an existential threat from global warming.

India's National Action Plan on Climate Change, adopted in June 2008 drew some criticism on account of its timing – just a week prior to the G-8 summit in To-kyo, when a stocktaking of progress in the fight against climate change was expected to be undertaken. One of the critiques was the absence of baseline data, since the last year for which complete data were available was 1994. [35]

This lacuna has since been remedied with the Ministry of Environment and For-ests (MoEF) in May 2010 issuing an updated inventory of India's GHG emissions. [36] The results show that India ranks fifth in the league of GHG polluters, behind the U. S., China, the European Union and Russia. Both the U. S. and China have four times India's volume of emissions. The study also points to a decline in the e-missions intensity of India's GDP growth by more than 30% between the two refer-ence periods, i. e., 1994 and 2007. The official target now is to reduce emissions intensity of GDP growth by another 20 to 25% by 2020.

The claim of a decline in emissions intensity needs to be seriously interrogated. Is this real in the sense that the techniques and processes thatIndia has adopted are in-herently less extravagant in terms of carbon emissions? Or does this supposed decline originate in the disequalising pattern of growth that India experienced through the two decades of liberalisation? Would this reduction in GHG emission relative to GDP have been achieved if all economic strata and social classes had partaken of the growth process in this period? In other words, is India anywhere near discovering an alternative paradigm of development that all sections of the country could benefit from, without unacceptable – and potentially catastrophic – environmental conse-quences?

India's ardour in embracing the Clean Development Mechanism (CDM) process created under the Kyoto Protocol, does not testify to a deeply held faith in the viability of the low-carbon growth path it has putatively embarked on. The most recent annual report of the Ministry of Environment and Forests (MoEF) records 1, 551 approvals by the national authority empowered to certify CDM projects.[37] Not all these have been registered by the CDM Executive Board, but they are estimated to have the potential to generate 627 million units of what is the newly minted currency of global carbon transactions: the Certified Emissions Reduction (CER). The MoEF has priced this currency – which is hard to touch and feel and has no existence outside the esoteric universe of the newly created tribe of carbon accountants – very conservatively, at US $ 10 per unit.

India's salience in the global CDM market is a matter of considerable satisfaction for the MoEF. As it puts the matter: "478 out of the total 2011 projects registered by the CDM Executive Board (as of January 2010) are from India, (which) is the second highest by any country in the world".[38]

Carbon trading as inaugurated under theKyoto protocol, is an arcane process, considerably more difficult to comprehend for the average intelligence than the global financial markets. Its key attribute is counter-factuality. A project's contribution to e-missions reduction is assessed against what might have happened if it had not been established. If degraded forest land were to be allowed to remain as is, what would be the total mass of carbon added to the atmosphere? How would this compare to the e-missions burden if that land were to be afforested? How much of a contribution to carbon containment would an urban solid waste processing system make, if it were to produce energy and soil compost, rather than allow the solid wastes to fester and de-compose?

To berecognised by the CDM Executive Board, the project would have to demonstrate an "additionality" in terms of carbon containment and also establish that without CDM funds, it would make no economic sense. The project would also need to be one that is implemented voluntarily, not as a legal compulsion.

Thus a municipal wastes disposal plant, which should be a requirement in all urbancentres, will under the CDM philosophy, become a source of carbon credits that could be sold in the global futures market and could indeed, be bought up by a polluting industry in the U. S. or China to evade obligatory caps on its own emissions. [39] A power plant in Kansas city in the U. S. , should its management feel disinclined to check emissions could instead, purchase the carbon credits created by an urban waste disposal plant in Kolhapur in India. The Kansas power operator evades its responsibility by subsidising the Kolhapur citizen's evasion of his civic duty.

A serious approach towards climate change would focus on evolving alternate technologies and processes that are environment-friendly, supportive of mass livelihoods and relatively less resource-intensive. A country that is aware of its long-term interests would consider these options with appropriate seriousness, rather than immerse itself enthusiastically in a corrupt web of international transactions promoted by the world's biggest polluters, in league with financial institutions with a record of sharp practices. There are ritualistic statements about reorienting India's national science and technology system in a fashion that is more reponsive to the new developmental paradigm, but few concrete moves to make that a reality.

11

Nuclear deal and after: diminished credibility?

It is an index ofIndia's priorities in this respect, that nuclear power is being pursued as the appropriate response to the challenge of climate change. This perception has in turn led to a number of strategic choices, that have deeply impinged on the terms of India's engagement with the developing world that it once had legitimate claims to lead.

In 2006, the Planning Commission in its mid-term appraisal of the Tenth Five Year Plan (X FYP) put out a rather bleak assessment of the performance of the nuclear power sector and attributed its shortfalls entirely to the failure to discover new sources of minerals that could be processed into nuclear fuel. This was the first that the public at large was hearing of a shortage of atomic minerals in the country, since the story that the Department of Atomic Energy (DAE) had been eagerly fostering since the 1950s was that India had sufficient resources to fuel an ambitious three-stage nuclear powerprogramme that would go from first generation heavy-water reactors, to fast-breeders based on plutonium, to thorium-fuelled reactors, within a few decades.

The Planning Commission summed up its assessment of the prospects of nuclear power, with a telling observation: "Nuclear energy remains an important tool for decarbonising the Indian energy sector".[40]

It was far from agreed then that the nuclear fuel cycle was a viable remedy for all the ills of the carbon fuel cycle. But this perception, as also the security anxieties that followedIndia's nuclear explosive tests of May 1998, ensured that much of India's international diplomatic effort was devoted in the months that followed, towards building up nuclear energy capacity while retaining sufficient flexibility under international covenants to build up an infinitely flexible arsenal of destructive nuclear weapons.

In July 2005, Prime MinisterManmohan Singh visited the U. S. capital and agreed a joint declaration with U. S. President George Bush that seemingly injected India into the exclusive orbit of recognised nuclear weapons states. This was achieved through a diplomatic contrivance by which India and the U. S. created a point on the international geostrategic map that till then did not exist. The joint statement adopted by Manmohan Singh and George Bush referred to India as a "responsible state with advanced nuclear technology", which should "acquire the same benefits and advantages as other such states". In effect, this created a special niche exclusively for India, in the limbo between the nuclear haves and have-nots.

Bush's visit to India in March 2006 was the occasion to put the finishing touches on the accord. If the deal that was agreed then succeeded in calming several of the anxieties suffered by unilateralists within the DAE, its international repercussions were something else. Pakistan's Foreign Minister warned darkly that the whole Nuclear Non-Proliferation Treaty (NPT) would "unravel" since it was "only a matter of time before other countries [began] to act the same way (as India)."

India's bonding with the U. S. also evoked deep suspicions in circles not known to be traditional bastions of hostility. *The Guardian* in London, for one, commented editorially, that the nuclear agreement between India and the U. S. was "about breaking rules and expecting others to abide by them". More picturesquely put, it was about "preaching temperance from the barstool". Indians may well delight in the bargain they had driven, said the newspaper, but there were likely to be some "thoughtful smiles" in Iran and North Korea as the "wider implications" sank in. [41]

In advance of the Bush visit, the *New York Times* observed that despite all the accompanying froth, the presidential passage to India was "built around a bad nuclear deal". With the deal consummated, the newspaper commented rather acidly, that Bush was turning out to be Iran's best friend. His adventure in Iraq, launched on flimsy and fabricated evidence, had only transformed that country into a satellite of the Islamic Republic next door. And his deal with India sent "exactly the wrong message" when Washington was scheduled to "refer Iran's case to the United Nations Security Council for further action". Iran's hopes of thwarting a global consensus on its nuclear programme rested on "convincing the rest of the world that the West [was] guilty of a double standard on nuclear issues", commented the *New York Times*. And in this respect, Bush "might as well have tied a pretty red bow around his India nuclear deal and mailed it as a gift to Tehran". [42]

Since then, India went through an arduous route to obtain a nuclear deal tailored to its particular mix of ambitions and anxieties. The Bush administration in the U. S. was well disposed but it took an extra effort to obtain the sanction of the U. S. Congress. This effort involved voting repeatedly against Iran in the councils of the International Atomic Energy Agency and defying the collective commonsense of the Non-Aligned Movement (NAM) , of which India was a founder and one-time leader. In global disarmament negotiations, India is now considered an interloper, a nation willing to sacrifice long-held principle in pursuit of national security chimeras.

12

A problem of image

Visitors toIndia in current times are unlikely to miss a pervasive new mood of aggressive self-assertion among the people who matter, a certain supreme complacence that "we" have arrived on the world stage and cannot any longer be denied a merited place at the high table in global councils. Suggestions that the celebration might be premature, are brusquely dismissed. Observations that a country with quite widespread evidence of human deprivation and numerous social fractures could not afford complacence on this scale are dismissed as voices from the past, born in minds still shackled by outmoded habits of thought.

Civil society groups in general have remained critical of this aggressive new mood. But little heed was paid to these dissenting voices within. India is now nearing the end of what can only be called a grand coming out party. After much heartburn in the run-up, the final accounts tally from the 19th Commonwealth Games hosted in the national capital city of Delhi, seems to indicate a small positive balance in terms of national prestige. The economic impact though is another matter since there is yet no indication that the enormous public investments that went into hosting the games will engender any of the expected positive spinoffs in terms of private sector gains. The human and social cost at which the CWG was brought to India still remains to be tallied. Recent action under the RTI law has revealed that the government both in Delhi and at the Union level, diverted funds meant for social welfare spending of benefit for the disadvantaged, to preparing facilities for the CWG. [43] International media coverage meanwhile, reports that India has forgotten its poor and disadvantaged in a headlong rush towards global power status. [44]

Just a month ahead of the CWG, the Indian administration wasriven by a blame – game over the evident mess that has been made of the preparations. Allegations of serious malfeasance flew thick and fast. The clear and present danger was seemingly averted, that the debutante ball marking India's emergence on the world stage, would be transformed into a testament of overblown ambitions failing the encounter with harsh realities. But many hard questions still remain unanswered.

Sukumar Muralidharan

October 13, 2010

Note

[1] A "millionaire" here is defined as an individual with personal disposablewealth in excess of US $ 1 million, apart from his or her primary residential property.

[2] See the report on the Finance Minister's statements in Kolkata in "Right to Health, Right to Food Next on Centre's agenda, says Pranab", *The Hindu*, August 9, 2010, p. 10; extracted on August 9 from: http://www.hindu.com/2010/08/09/stories/2010080956811000.htm.

[3] An interview with the principal author of the OPHDI study is available in "Media Hype and the Reality of the New India", *The Hindu*, Delhi, July 20, 2010, page 12, extracted on August 28 from: http://www.thehindu.com/opinion/interview/article523817.ece. Further details are available through the website of the OPHDI: http://www.ophi.org.uk/policy/multidimensional – poverty – index/.

[4] Some of these issues have been presented in a useful summarised form, though

one that is partial towards his own viewpoint by Angus Deaton. See Angus Deaton and Valerie Kozel, "Data and Dogma: The Great Indian Poverty Debate", at: http://papers. ssrn. com/sol3/papers. cfm? abstract_ id = 593864.

[5]The report of the expert group chaired by the economist Suresh Tendulkar is available at the website of the Planning Commission: http://www. planningcommission. nicin/eg_ poverty. htm.

[6] Government of India, Ministry of Finance, *Economic Survey* 2009 – 10, Delhi, March 2010, pp. 270 – 1. Obviously, if the physical analogy were to beextended, growth has proved a very poor power source for human development. All prime movers suffer some losses in efficiency when converted into final usable energy output. But all prime movers have clearly quantified indicesof efficiency, such as a diesel engine that runs a locomotive will have anefficiency of 50% in the best conditions. If economic growth is the power source behind human development, we are yet to obtain an adequate index ofits efficiency in providing this final output.

[7] See the two articles by Jean Dreze and associates in *Frontline* issues dated July 27, 2007 and February 27, 2009, available at: http://www. frontline. in/fl2414/stories/20070727001804100. htm and http://frontline. in/fl2604/stories/20090227 260410100. htm.

[8]Institute of Applied Manpower Research, "All-India Report on Evaluation of NREGA: A Survey of 20 Districts", Delhi, 2009, available at: http://www. planningcommission. nic. in/reports/genrep/rep_ NREGA_ 03 – 08 – 2009. pdf.

[9] India, Ministry of Finance, Economic Survey, 2009 – 10, pp. 3, 64.

[10] India, Ministry of Finance, Economic Survey, 2002 – 03, p. 80.

[11] Figures available from the website of the Food Corporation of India, extracted from: http://fciweb. nic. in/stock _ management/Stock _ WheatRIce_ Central _ Pool. pdf.

[12] See "Abandoning godowns, FCI opts for the open", *Mint* (Delhi Edition), July 28, 2010, page 6, available at this writing at: http://www. livemint. com/

2010/07/27193718/Abandoning – godowns – FCI – opts – f. html? atype = tp. Foodgrain rot on account of poor storage, corruption and negligence by the Food Corporation of India (FCI) is surely not a newstory. But it is important to note the media's most recent effort tohighlight an issue of vital consequence for the country's poor, that oftengoes unreported.

[13] See for instance, the 2009 version of the annual publication of the FAO, *State of Food Insecurity in the World*, chapter titled "Towards Eliminating Hunger".

[14] There is by now a fairly well-established scholarly consensus on this. For an empirical analysis, see Himanshu, "Recent Trends in Poverty and Inequality: Some Preliminary Results", Economic and Political Weekly, February 10, 2007, pp. 497 – 508.

[15] Kaushik Basu, "India's Dilemmas: The Political Economy of Policymakingin a Globalised World", Ecoomic and Political Weekly, February 2, 2008, p. 54.

[16] See this writer's "Developing Resistance", in Frontline, August 30 – September 12, 2003, available at this writing at: http: //www. frontline. in/fl2018/stories/20030912001804500. htm.

[17] Extracted from the official web portal of the President of Russia, at http: // archive. kremlin. ru/eng/text/docs/2009/06/217963. shtml. Also see the front-page report in The Hindu, July 17, 2009: "BRIC should create conditions for fairer world order", available at this writing athttp: //www. hindu. com/2009/06/17/ stories/2009061759641000. htm.

[18] "PM against merger of IBSA, BRIC blocs", The Times of India, Delhi, April 17, 2010, extracted on August 12 from: http: //timesofindia. indiatimes. com/india/PM – against – merger – of – IBSA – BRIC – blocs/articleshow/5823437. cms.

[19] "11 panels from India, four other nations attempt Doha revival", the Economic Times, August 4, 2010, extracted at: http: //economictimes. indiatimes. com/news/economy/foreign – trade/11 – panels – from – India – 4 – other – nations-

attempt – Doha – revival/articleshow/6258975. cms.

[20] Ashok Gulati and Anil Sharma, "Subsidy Syndrome in Indian Agriculture", Economic and Political Weekly, September 30, 1995, pp. A 93 – A 102.

[21] Kaushik Basu, op. cit. .

[22] There is an element of ambiguity about this mode of classification, which is one among three schemes used to report public sector spending, the others being capital versus revenue expenditure, and plan versus non-plan.

[23] See "Performance of Private Corporate Business Sector, 2007 – 08", in Reserve Bank of India Bulletin, September 2008, pp. 1511 – 30.

[24] K. S. Chalapati Rao and Biswajit Dhar, "Accelerating India's FDI Inflows: Conceptual and Definitional Issues", Working Paper, Institute for Studies in Industrial Development, Delhi, April 2010. I am grateful to Dr Chalapati Rao for providing me access to a pre-publication draft of this paper.

[25] The data are drawn from relevant volumes of the RBI *Handbook of Statistics on the Indian Economy*. The market capitalisation figures usedare for the terminal date of the relevant year, i. e. , March 31. To the extent that these are a stock magnitude and the GDP is an annual flow, thetwo may not be commensurable. The ratio of the two is used purely forillustrative purposes.

[26] The National Housing Bank (NHB) introduced an index of nation-wideresidential property prices in 2007. Called the NHB Residex, the index hasbeen updated till December 2009 and shows that beginning with the secondhalf of 2008, there has been an erosion of housing values in several majorcities, and most especially so in Bangalore and Hyderabad. Values stagnated through 2008 in Delhi and Mumbai, before resuming a moderately-paced increase in 2009. Kolkata and Chennai values have continued to rise, as also in the lower rung urban centres of Bhopal and Faridabad. The second-rung metros like Pune and Ahmedabad, and major urban centres like Jaipurand Kochi, all had sharp downturns in real estate values in 2008, followedby a year of indifferent performance in 2009. (See the most updatedstatistics at: http: //

www. nhb. org. in/Residex/Data&Graphs. php). Unfortunately, figures are not available for the peak of the boom, but various informal estimates, based on surveys of housing market players, put the rate of growth of prices in Delhi and Bangalore of about 26 to 28% between 2003 and 2006 and between 10 and 15% in 2007 (See: http://www. globalpropertyguide. com/Asia/India/Price – History).

[27] On the impact of the "wealth effect" on consumption levels, see the Federal Reserve Bank of San Francisco, "Disentangling the Wealth Effect: Some International Evidence", Newsletter Number 2007 – 02, January 18, 2007, available at this writing at: http://www. frbsf. org/publications/economics/letter/2007/el2007 – 02. pdf.

[28] Government of India, Ministry of Finance, *Economic Survey* 2009 – 10, Delhi, February 2010, page 124.

[29] See Paul Krugman's column in the *New York Times*, August 26, 2010, "This Is Not a Recovery", (available at: http://www. nytimes. com/2010/08/27/opinion/27krugman. html? hp) for a summation of the case against viewing the current status of the U. S. economy as anything approaching a recovery.

[30] An instance that comes readily to mind is the aftermath of the 2004 general elections to the Indian parliament, when it became evident that the new coalition that would soon take office, would be dependent on the parties of the left for its parliamentary majority. A remark by a left political leader that his party opposes the disinvestment of shares in public sector enterprises, led to a sharp fall in equity values that had captains of industry calling for an explicit disavowal from all the other main coalition partners.

[31] Raghuraman G. Rajan, *Fault Lines: How hidden fractures still threaten the world economy*, Collins Business, Delhi, 2010, p. 209.

[32] See his column "Paralysis at the Fed", *The New York Times*, August 12, 2010, available at: http://www. nytimes. com/2010/08/13/opinion/13krugman. html? ref = paulkrugman.

[33] The study, as also much other relevant material on climate change, canbe found at the Delhi Science Forum website: http://www.delhiscienceforum.net/.

[34] The phrase is attributed to the U.S. Senator John Warner, in Eric Pooley, *The Climate War*, Hyperion, New York, 2010, chapter 1.

[35] Praful Bidwai, *An India that can say Yes: A Climate – Responsible Development Agenda for Copenhagen and Beyond*, Heinrich Boell Foundation, New Delhi, 2009.

[36] The report can be viewed at the website of India's Ministry ofEnvironment and Forests, http://moef.nic.in/downloads/public – information/Report _ INC-CA.pdf.

[37] Government of India, Ministry of Environment and Forests, Annual Report2009 – 10, p. 269.

[38] Ibid, p. 270.

[39] See the very important article by Mark Schapiro, "Conning the Climate", *Harper's*, February 2010, pp. 31 – 9.

[40] Planning Commission, Mid-Term Appraisal of the Tenth Five-Year Plan, Delhi, 2006, page 339 (available at: http://www.planningcommission.nic.in/plans/mta/midterm/english – pdf/chapter – 10.pdf).

[41] "Bush and the Bomb", *The Guardian*, Leader, March 4, 2006.

[42] "Iran's Best Friend", *The New York Times*, editorial, March 5, 2006, available at: http://www.nytimes.com/2006/03/05/opinion/05sun1.html? _ r = 1.

[43] See "Rs 744 crore Dalit funds diverted for Games" in the *Times of India*, July 16, 2010, page 1, available at: http://timesofindia.indiatimes.com/city/delhi/Rs – 744cr – dalit – fund – diverted – for – Games/articleshow/6173912.cms.

[44] " 'Shining India' makes its poor pay price of Commonwealth Games", *The Guardian*, July 11, 2010, available at: http://www.guardian.co.uk/world/2010/jul/11/slum – school – india – commonwealth – games.

图书在版编目（CIP）数据

印度与世界：对融入世界新模式的认识／（印）莫拉里塔兰著；
刘小雪译．—北京：社会科学文献出版社，2014.3
  ISBN 978 - 7 - 5097 - 5638 - 6

Ⅰ. ①印… Ⅱ. ①莫…②刘… Ⅲ. ①印度 - 研究 Ⅳ. ①D735.1

中国版本图书馆 CIP 数据核字（2014）第 021873 号

印度与世界：对融入世界新模式的认识

著　者／〔印〕苏库马尔·莫拉里塔兰（Sukumar Muralidharan）
译　者／刘小雪

出　版　人／谢寿光
出　版　者／社会科学文献出版社
地　　　址／北京市西城区北三环中路甲 29 号院 3 号楼华龙大厦
邮政编码／100029

责任部门／全球与地区问题出版中心（010）59367004　　责任编辑／高明秀　许玉燕
电子信箱／bianyibu@ ssap. cn　　　　　　　　　　　　责任校对／张彦彬
项目统筹／高明秀　许玉燕　　　　　　　　　　　　　　责任印制／岳　阳
经　　销／社会科学文献出版社市场营销中心（010）59367081　59367089
读者服务／读者服务中心（010）59367028

印　　装／三河市尚艺印装有限公司
开　　本／787mm×1092mm　1/16　　　　　印　张／7.5
版　　次／2014 年 3 月第 1 版　　　　　　　字　数／112 千字
印　　次／2014 年 3 月第 1 次印刷
书　　号／ISBN 978 - 7 - 5097 - 5638 - 6
定　　价／59.00 元